THE ROMANIAN SENTIMENT OF BEING

Before you start to read this book, take this moment to think about making a donation to punctum books, an independent non-profit press,

@ https://punctumbooks.com/support/

If you're reading the e-book, you can click on the image below to go directly to our donations site. Any amount, no matter the size, is appreciated and will help us to keep our ship of fools afloat. Contributions from dedicated readers will also help us to keep our commons open and to cultivate new work that can't find a welcoming port elsewhere. Our adventure is not possible without your support.

Vive la Open Access.

Fig. 1. Detail from Hieronymus Bosch, *Ship of Fools* (1490–1500)

First published in 2022 by punctum books, Earth, Milky Way.
https://punctumbooks.com

Originally published in Romanian by Editura Eminescu, Bucharest, as *Sentimentul românesc al ființei* © 1978 by Constantin Noica

ISBN-13: 978-1-68571-038-5 (print)
ISBN-13: 978-1-68571-039-2 (ePDF)

DOI: 10.53288/0355.1.00

LCCN: 2022934727
Library of Congress Cataloging Data is available from the Library of Congress

Book design: Vincent W.J. van Gerven Oei
Cover photograph: Constantin Brâncusi, *Poarta sărutului* (*The Gate of the Kiss*, 1938), Târgu Jiu, Romania. Photograph by fusion-of-horizons on *Flickr*.

punctumbooks
spontaneous acts of scholarly combustion

HIC SVNT MONSTRA

Constantin Noica

The Romanian Sentiment of Being

translated by Octavian and Elena Gabor

Contents

Translators' Note

In 1978, the philosopher Emil Cioran (1911–95), friend of Constantin Noica (1909–87), wrote him a short letter. The epistle ended with some words about Noica's newly published volume, *The Romanian Sentiment of Being*: "Your last book is excellent; the only thing is that it could have been called just as well The Paraguayan Sentiment of Being. In your place, I would return to Logic: where, if not there, can one rave better?"[1] Cioran's irony stems from a thought that many may have when faced with this volume: why would there be any interest in a book about the sentiment of being of a people? And how can a people's sentiment give us an answer to a question as old as Western philosophy—what is being? Finally, what would make the Romanian sentiment of being, even if it gave some insight about being itself, be more special than the Paraguayan, French, Vietnamese, Nigerian, or American ones? Indeed, nothing makes them more special than others. But this is not to say that they are not unique. And, if they are unique, revealing their uniqueness may increase the understanding of being that we as humanity have. Noica says, "But every language is, after all, the wisdom of the world in one of its versions. This wisdom of the world needs the particular wisdom of language in order to explore reality

1 Emil Cioran, *Scrisori către cei de acasă* [*Letters for Those Who Remained Home*] (Bucharest: Humanitas, 1995), 310.

in all the ways and to transfer its knowledge into words."[2] This book, then, is an attempt to understand reality, the same reality, through the cultural wisdom of a people as it is expressed in Romanian language.

The fact that we deal with the deep structure of a language makes this translation very difficult. When we approached philosopher Gabriel Liiceanu, one of the most prominent of Noica's disciples, about the translation of this volume, he gave us his approval with these words: "The project requires a courage that borders craziness; one cannot imagine something more difficult, something that is almost untranslatable. How do you want to translate into English the inner depths of the Romanian language?" These words have come back to us every day we worked on this project. Nevertheless, we persevered. After all, translating the Romanian sentiment of being into English is what we do every day: both of us have grown up in the Romanian culture that shaped our being in this world, and we live as who we are in an English-speaking country. Nevertheless, this also means that, at times, we left some Romanian words untranslated, such as the preposition întru. When we did so, we explained this choice as thoroughly as we were able, providing, at the same time, various approximations in English.

This is the second book of Constantin Noica published by punctum books. The previous one, *Pray for Brother Alexander*, translated by Octavian Gabor, appeared in 2018. In 2009 Alistair Ian Blyth published his two translations of Noica's works, *Becoming within Being* (Marquette University Press) and *Six Maladies of the Contemporary Spirit* (University of Plymouth Press).

Noica remains one of the most important figures of Romanian philosophy of the twentieth century. He was considered an anti-revolutionary thinker by the communist regime because of his writings on Hegel's *Phenomenology of the Spirit*. He spent years in house arrest and in political prison, moments that were captured in his prison memoir, *Pray for Brother Alexander*. For

2 This volume, 58.

more on his life and philosophy, see Octavian Gabor's "Constantin Noica's 'Becoming within Being' and 'Meno's Paradox.'"[3]

The volume contains two other works in the appendix. Noica analyzes them in detail in the volume, and we thought that adding them here would enrich the readers' experience. The first is the famous poem "Luceafărul" ["The Evening Star"], by poet Mihai Eminescu (1850–89), in Octavian Gabor's translation. The second work is a well known Romanian story in the version of Petre Ispirescu, "Ageless Youth and Deathless Life." This story was translated in entirety by Elena Gabor. All footnotes were written by Octavian Gabor, unless otherwise noted.

We remain indebted to Dana LaCourse Munteanu who had the original idea to translate this volume and who offered us helpful suggestions during its completion.

We are infinitely grateful to Lily Brewer, this book's copyeditor, who embraced the spirit of the volume and whose gentle comments and suggestions improved it.

— Octavian and Elena Gabor

3 Octavian Gabor, "Constantin Noica's 'Becoming within Being' and 'Meno's Paradox,'" in *A Handbook to Classical Reception in Eastern and Central Europe*, eds. Zara Martirosova Torlone, Dana Lacourse Munteanu, and Dorota Deutsch (Chichester: Wiley-Blackwell, 2017), 300–311.

Preface

If a nourishing plant were to grow on Romanian soil and were not found any other place, we would be responsible for it. If words and meanings that can enrich a human's thought emerged in our language and did not emerge in others' speech or thought, we are still bound to give an account for them.[1] Such a word is *întru*;[2] such a meaning is that of "being." In fact, the special meaning of "being" in our language is perhaps the work of the various meanings of *întru*, which came to express being as if from *within*, suggesting that "to be" means "to be *întru* some-

1 We translated in two different ways the Romanian expression, *a da socoteală*. In Romanian, the expression means, at the same time, "to give an account" of something and also "be responsible" for something. In the first sentence, we used "being responsible" and, here, "giving an account," hoping that in this way we would encapsulate both meanings.

2 Noica uses the Romanian word *întru* to express what in English can be rendered by using both "within" and "toward." *Întru* originates from the Latin prefix *intro* ("to the inside," "inward"; for example, the English word *introduction*: *intro*, which means "inward," and *ducere*, which means "to lead"). Alistair Ian Blyth has translated the title of *Devenirea întru ființă* as *Becoming within Being* (Marquette University Press, 2009). Noica's *întru* captures the idea that becoming does not only take place within a nature of something, but also always toward a nature. See for this Octavian Gabor, "Noica's 'Becoming withing Being' and 'Meno's Paradox'," in *A Handbook to Classical Reception in Eastern and Central Europe*, eds. Zara Martirosova Torlone, Dana LaCourse Munteanu, and Dorota Dutsch (Chichester: Wiley-Blackwell, 2017), 309–11.

thing," so to be in and not fully in something, to rest but also to aspire, to close but also to open. Being was thus taken out from its fixity, and it trembled. But if it didn't tremble, would it truly *be*? What kind of being is that in which there is no place for a vibration and thus no place for becoming?

Something new seemed to stem from here, diversifying being and unsettling it, instead of leaving it unitary and calm as it seemed when viewed from outside. Being has thus lost its gravity, together with its absolute character. For our infuse, speculative sensibility,[3] being has a good margin of freedom and, in our terms, a delicate nature. This does not mean lack of responsibility regarding the problem of being but rather the establishment of an open notion of being.

Those who began with the gravity of being and its closed notion arrived at nothingness and the absurd, as it happened in some contemporary orientations in the West. The delicate nature of being, however, does not give the sentiment of its fragility but rather that of its universal presence, even if at different levels and intensities. We try then to speak of a specific Romanian sentiment of being, just as it could be said that the German soul has a specific sentiment of becoming, the Russian one a specific sentiment of space, and the American one a specific sentiment of efficiency.

Just as Eminescu[4] said about our language that "this language came out of the shrouds of the past," we could also say that the Romanian notion of being comes out today from the shrouds of the past and of the language itself. These pages, at least, attempt to bring light to this thing. This cannot be a philosophical work since our language or our fairytales and creations do not shroud

3 We use the first-person plural whenever Noica refers to the Romanian culture, perspective, or sensibility. Noica uses the same first-person plural when he refers to himself, which is the usual academic Romanian custom. In all of these situations, we translated his expressions by using first-person singular.

4 Mihai Eminescu (1850–89) is considered the Romanian national poet. Noica discusses in this volume one of his most famous poems: "Luceafărul" ("The Evening Star").

a speculative contemplation from where we could decipher the thought of being; it seems that a philosophical view may be at stake for Eminescu only, but it is not an organized one even in his case. However, if I do not have as purpose to make this volume a philosophical treatise about the notion of being, one could attempt to write such a treatise as a continuation of these interpretations. I've written about some Romanian words,[5] and I now write about the gain they brought in the discussion on being. Subsequently, I imagine an attempt about being that would no longer be dependent on the Romanian words and meanings.[6] But it will also be born, if it succeeds, from the abundance of these words and meanings.[7]

— The Author

5 Prior to the publication of *Sentimentul românesc al ființei* [*The Romanian Sentiment of Being*] (Bucharest: Editura Eminescu, 1978), Noica also wrote *Pagini despre sufletul românesc* [*Pages on the Romanian Soul*] (Bucharest: Colecția Luceafărul, 1944), *Rostirea filozofică românească* [*Romanian Philosophical Utterance*] (Bucharest: Editura științifică, 1970), and *Creație și frumos în rostirea românească* [*Creation and Beauty in Romanian Utterance*] (Bucharest: Editura Eminescu, 1973).

6 In 1981, Noica published *Devenirea întru ființă* (Bucharest: Editura științifică), which, as mentioned above, was translated in English by Alistair Ian Blyth, *Becoming within Being*.

7 Noica's note in the Romanian edition: Some pages from this writing were published between 1970–76 as articles in *Steaua*. The introduction was published in the review *Transilvania* in 1974.

Introduction

As any being in this world, a people is a good closure that opens itself. The Romanian people's determinations *întru* itself are well known. Its openings have not yet ceased.

Our language has a special word for a closure that opens itself, the preposition *întru*, for which it is difficult to find an equivalent in the great European languages. It is not necessary, however, to reveal the nuances of *întru* to a speaker of Romanian. At most, one can remind him that, having its origin in the Latin adverb *intro*, which means "inside," our preposition added the meaning of "toward" (*în spre*), which provides a good tension that is of the essence of the spirit, the tension of being *in* something (in a horizon, in a system) and of aspiring toward that thing at the same time.

Thus, by the determinations of its own history, our civilization was *întru* a given space. It didn't swarm like the Hellenic civilization, giving its own colonies on all neighboring shores; it didn't approximate its space, like the German civilization; it didn't colonize others, like the Anglo-Saxon civilization. It dwelt in the space around the Carpathians. There were other people who passed through this space; but they only passed through. We remained within it. And we stayed so well *întru* it that some migrating peoples had to settle around it, while others melted in our being.

As it was *întru* a space, our civilization also was *întru* a language, the Latin. Our neighbors from below, from left, and from right[1] gave us many and admirable words, but all of them were caught in this language of Latin birth. When, in the nineteenth century, our connections with the rest of the world were remade, the Latinity of our language was found again not only in birth, but also in act, in an absorption — one that seemed to be done from its own storerooms — of many words from its mother tongue, Latin, and its sister tongue, French.

Our civilization, even at the level of the spirit, took place over centuries preponderantly *întru* something, *întru* nature. We cannot call this pantheism, as it was attempted at times, but it isn't about a common experience of nature either. Our spiritual life has taken place *întru* the comprehensive and meanings-filled reality of Mother nature, giving us that sentiment of the concrete real that is mentioned by all who know the Romanian soul. While other peoples[2] oppose the spirit to nature, the two of them interwove here, and the extreme strength of the spirit has never transformed into its excesses.

When our civilization rose to culture, it did not create everything again, but it was, just as it was before nature, *întru* given historical cultures. The vain temptation of total novelty did not appear among us. We knew to bring novelty *întru* that which was proper to us historically. This is why it could be said, for example, that the originality of our art consists in giving a "harmonious synthesis," so in making novelty to not be in the thing itself but *întru* it.

It has been said that our civilization is between two worlds. Isn't it *întru* two worlds? We are between the Near East and the Far East (in an admirable posthumous page, Blaga[3] says defini-

1 Noica means South, West, and East. The use of below, left, and right suggests looking at a map.

2 We use the term "people" here to mean "all the men, women, and children who live in a particular country, or who have the same culture or language" (*Cambridge Dictionary*, s.v., "people").

3 Lucian Blaga (1895–1961) is one of the most important Romanian philosophers and poets of the twentieth century.

tory things about our openness toward Indian culture), and the West. Neither of them has put their stamp on us. Just as we mediate geographically, couldn't we also mediate spiritually?

In any case, our civilization has the privilege to be *întru* a tradition that can represent an active factor. Overwhelmed by the number of past centuries, some peoples could let their traditions active only in a small measure, and so for them living in the spirit of tradition or in the spirit of modernity was an unceasing tearing. We can continue to be *întru* what we have been, going forward together with the times.

On the basis of this tradition, the Romanian people has a larger encounter than others with the values of the spirit. In itself, tradition means keeping that which was good in the past *întru* spirit. However, such a positive placement *întru* the things of the spirit could have been translated more by a closure, regardless of how beautiful it may have been, as, for example, a closure into a folkloric culture only. We had the seventeenth century, though, the one of great personalities. Then, the second half of the nineteenth century also gave great cultural personalities. In fact, the nature of this folkloric culture, just as our encounter with values, does not raise against the novelties of the age, but they interweave unexpectedly with them.

It may be, though, that an age needs to engage its terrible novelties *întru* something. In this sense, our spiritual experience could teach us how to be ourselves *întru* today's world and how to be useful to such a renovating world.

This time, however, our openings must be significant, and they truly show themselves to be so. Of course, the majority of nations[4] attempts a good opening within their space. Similarly, they also attempt an opening of their languages, through culture. But not all communities still have a good opening toward nature at the time of technology during the scientific revolution, nor do they have a good experience of tradition and val-

4 "Nations" translates here the Romanian term, *popoare*, which was rendered as "peoples" above. In this case, however, "nations" seemed to work better.

ues. What is certainly not given to other communities today is the possible opening *întru* the two worlds: the West with the Extreme West, and the Near East with the Extreme Orient, two worlds that are about to meet. There is no other place where the situation of the "closure that can open itself" appears with so much historical pregnancy: in their encounter, two massive worlds close a community which, instead of being crushed by them, as at a crossroad, can open itself towards them and, especially, open them toward each other.

We could include here, with a positive role, our affinity with the novelties of the age, while maintaining values that are older than the age.

If you wonder why this people succeeded in its self-affirmations in the past and why it maintains in today's Europe the chances of some good openings, this is a possible answer: because it has an appropriate encounter with being. Being does not show itself in the same manner to anyone; not all people perceive being as a sort of "being *întru*." There are consciousnesses for which being is a sort of "being in," so being in something that is absolute, already given, unwavering. Man's possible collapses spring partly from here.[5]

But being is clearly a sort of "being *întru*." It is sufficient to consider the being of man. As human, each one of us is determined by an individual nature in which he feels restricted but by which he has the duty to open himself toward that which is human. Each human belongs to a national being and a social being by which he can and must open himself toward the universal.

---

5 We have chosen to use "man" whenever there are references to classical problems in Western philosophy, such as, "what is man?" On the one hand, this approach helps to situate Noica's view in its proper historical context. On the other hand, it also helps to distinguish between various philosophical uses of a being of the human species. Thus, we use "man" whenever we refer to the abstract notion of a human being. We use "a human" to refer to an individual of the human species. "A human's being" designates the being or the nature of a human being in his or her particularity, while "the being of man" will designate the being of a human as human.

Similarly, any creature is limited, but in order *to be,* he must pass genuinely from a limitation that limits[6] to one that doesn't limit.

Întru, which suggests precisely such a limitation that doesn't limit, is actually a question. It seems to us that, at the first hour, we must feel being as a question and not as an answer. For man, everything starts from a question, truly speaking. This is why, in order to research the Romanian sentiment of being, it is appropriate to see if our way of questioning gives justice to the question and if it communicates something different than others' ways.

6 A limitation that creates boundaries.

I

The Horizon of the Question

When you receive an answer, you "are illuminated." On the contrary, when you ask a question, you "bring things into the light." Properly speaking, it is about illuminating things,[1] placing them in the light, in the sense that you are opening a horizon where things can appear clearly or not. The way in which you project the fascicule of light by questioning is the way in which you confront things, and the richness of the modes of interrogation is connected no more to the subtlety of an interrogating consciousness[2] than to the subtlety of the existent thing about which it questions. After all, why would you nuance your questions about a coarse reality? Reality itself must have various states, suggestions, inclinations, and declinations so that the questions' richness of nuances may have sense. This is why the ingenuity of the questions you can ask in Romanian language doesn't necessarily belong to the people who dwell here, who were not favored much by history, but rather to things, whose favor people knew how to see.

---

1 There is no real equivalent for the Romanian *o luminare* in English. Noica suggests that things become visible because of light. *Luminare* encompasses both aspects, that is, the visibility of things and the process of being made visible by light.

2 "An interrogating consciousness" is a human mind that approaches the world around it with questions.

1.

First, a question brings a *suspension*. Every thing in part and the world as a whole can be suspended by a question at a certain moment. With a question, the world neither is, nor does it stop being. And what seems to take place only within an interrogating consciousness — that the world is placed between parentheses "for me," or it exists in reality, but it is suspended and problematic only in my eyes — regards in fact the very basis of a thing. Is this thing real?[3] Isn't it shaken in its depth, or doesn't the interrogation about it show its shaking when the question sends it to its foundations, so to its rendering-it-possible?[4]

One does not need the question, "is it or is it not this way?" in order to indicate the fact that anything stays or has stayed under an initial insecurity; to send them to their original title of identity, it is enough to ask the question, "who is it?" or "what is it?" addressed to being or to a thing. It is a question that shakes a human anytime because it makes him pay attention to what he is ultimately.

Thus, since it is about a suspension, the oral question has an interrogative intonation in almost all languages, in this case by raising the tone. Speech itself enters in suspension by rising, in order to show that all things — the thought about a thing, the process of existence and knowledge, in a sense the thing itself — stay suspended prior to returning, as novelty or renewal, in the bosom of reality. A question regenerates reality.

---

3 In Romanian, one can ask whether something is without adding a predicate. We chose to translate the expression *este el?* with "is this real?" because it is the most neutral, to our minds. It can also be translated as "does this thing exist?" or "is this thing true?" This is the veridical sense of "to be" that also appears in Ancient Greek.

4 "Rendering-it-possible" translates *facerea lui cu putință*. The verb used in the Romanian expression also means "to make," and it suggests a thing's creation. *Facerea* is the name of the first book of the Bible, Genesis.

2.

Second, because it can regenerate part by part or fully, a question becomes an *în-doire*[5] about reality, so its duplication, in a sense its mirroring. Indeed, the question accompanies reality as a mirror, just as it accompanies the entire universe of utterances. Everything we assert can be placed under interrogation, similar to everything that is seen and exists.[6] Aristotle said about soul that it *is*, in a sense, all things,[7] having in mind its endless capacity to register and conceive them. A question, though, is all things in an even more precise sense: it suspends all of them and displays their images by mirroring. Just like in a mirror, the image from the question is overturned.

If in the case of the first feature of interrogation, the one of suspending things, the raising of intonation was significant for the uttered question, what's significant for the second feature is the fact that the question is asked by inverting the order of words. Again, in most languages, the interrogation can be done by placing the predicate before the subject (*bate vântul?*[8]) and perhaps by a reordering of the parts of the sentence. In a language that is somewhat mechanically developed, like English, the inversion brought by the question in the entire universe of utterances is revealed clearly, by the automatic way in which the

5 The Romanian term *îndoire* has two relevant meanings here. On the one hand, it can be translated as "folding in two." On the other hand, it also means "doubting."

6 Noica uses the verb "to be" here. See n. 3 above about the use of "to be" in Romanian.

7 Aristotle begins his *De Anima* by saying, "The knowledge of the soul admittedly contributes greatly to the advance of truth in general, and, above all, to our understanding of Nature, for the soul is in some sense the principle of animal life" (402a4–7). In Book III.8, he says again, "Let us now summarize our results about soul, and repeat that the soul is in a way all existing things" (431b20–21). For all Aristotelian quotes henceforth, we use *The Complete Works of Aristotle*, ed. Jonathan Barnes, 2 vols. (Princeton: Princeton University Press, 1984).

8 "Does the wind blow?" We left the expression in Romanian to show the order of the subject and the predicate. The verb is *bate* ("blows"), and the subject is *vântul* ("the wind").

interrogation is made: any affirmation is resumed, by the question, with the negation, and any negation by the affirmation. (*Vântul bate. Nu bate? Nu bate vântul. Bate?* ["The wind blows. Doesn't it? The wind doesn't blow. Does it?"]) When grammar tells us that the inversion of the composed verbal forms in languages like ours is archaic and regional (*Plăcutu-ți-a?*[9]), it forgets to add that the inversion is the essence of the question, which passes everything in its mirror.

3.

Third, it is still in the essence of *interrogation* to ally its negation or some negative formulations by the overturning that it proposes. The mechanism of interrogation in English has indeed something too mechanical within it. In various languages, beyond the fact that an interrogation is made by negating an affirmation, it can also be done by negating a negation, or at least with doubling it, using expressions such as, *Nu-i așa?* ("Isn't it?") or, in Romanian, *nu cumva? (Nu-i așa că nu bate vântul?* ["Isn't it true that the wind is not blowing?"]) Such expressions, and even simple negation, can come into play fully when it's about the universe of utterance and when it is about the universe of things or processes that are named and placed in suspension by a question, as it will soon be seen.

Indeed, having this capacity to make an ally of negation in form, interrogation risks to become negativity by its very content or at least by its function. Doubting[10] things can lead to their pure and simple negation. In any case, interrogation already shows that it does not accept to be only a reply to things, or, respectively, their suspension and mirroring. A question

9 This is an untranslatable expression. The meaning is, "Did you like it?" In Romanian, the verb used has as subject the object that is liked, as in Italian, for example, *Ti è piaciuto?* A possible rendering in English would be, "Was it pleasing to you?" In this particular case, the inversion is even more accentuated than in current use, *ți-a plăcut?*

10 *În-doire,* see n. 5.

about them and the question's return means in some cases — as common sense realized — their rejection. A certain "daimonic"[11] character of the question appears clearly, with the sense of possible denial. It is true, at times a question can have something daimonic in a neutral sense (as in Goethe's notion of the demonic): the suggestion that, around a thing, interrogativity can awaken a richness that cannot be contained in a rational way. This is what was found in the capacity of interrogation to suspend anything, respectively to mirror any real aspect. But now, with negation, it shows something of its more accused-demonic nature, in the measure that it can reach denial. This is what has always happened with skepticism, where a question is directly allied with negation, or it represents by itself an attempt of negation.

4.

However, the negativity of dissolution[12] is only an excess of interrogativity; what's more characteristic is the negativity of *indetermination*. Interrogativity goes beyond brute negation and finds itself as neutral opening. It does not prohibit, as absolute negation wants to do; on the contrary, it authorizes too much, as specific negation wants. When you are faced with a thing or process, you say, it is neither this nor that. But what is it? It is *some*thing, so that which it *will* be, just as the process takes place sometime, someplace, somehow, with all those indeterminate expressions connected with future, so clearly active in Romanian language.

Once again, this essential aspect of interrogativity is reflected in the forms of expression. If a question was made by raising the tone in the case of suspension, by inverting words in inverted mirroring, and by negating interrogative forms in the weaving

11 From the Greek *daimōn*. We chose "daimonic" and not "daimonian" because it suggests a closeness with "demonic," which is implied in Noica's use.

12 The Romanian word here is *desființare*, "un-being" something, canceling its being.

with negation, now, in the case of indetermination, the question is asked by specific formulas, which linguistics seems to record without explaining them.

This is how *cumva*[13] appears in our language, which could be associated to "no," but it can also be used freely ("Does the wind blow by any chance?"); there are also other form of interrogations that appear in our language, such as those derived from disjunctives, which clearly bring to light indetermination. In our language — not only in our language, but it happens here more richly — questions are asked with former disjunctive conjunctions or with others that became disjunctive for a moment, in their semantic evolution.

The interrogative *oare*[14] remains on first plan. By it, one can ask any question, be it total or partial. But, according to some linguists, *oare* comes from the Latin *hora,* hour, time. *Oară,* the dictionaries say (for example, Candrea and Densușianu's *Dicționar Etimologic*[15]), was first used as an adverb, meaning "now"; due to constructions of the type, *oară-oară,* meaning "now-now," as in the formula, "now one…now another," the disjunctive formula *ori-ori* ("either-or") was formulated, which could produce *ori* ("or") pure and simple, and so the disjunctive conjunction. (It is worth emphasizing here the richness of disjunctive formulas in our language, formulas that are not necessarily reduced to a simple alternative: *ori-ori, veri-veri, sau-sau, au-au, fie-fie, când-când, ici-ici, măcar-măcar, uneori-alteori.*[16])

13 *Cumva* is an adverb that indicates a mode of being. It can slightly change its meaning, depending on whether it is used in the interrogative or negative. In a question, it can be rendered with, "by any chance," as it can be seen in the parenthetical phrase. In a negative expression, such as *nu cumva bate vântul?,* it can be rendered as, "Isn't it the case that the wind is blowing?"

14 An adverb that strengthens the interrogative function of a sentence, but it also suggests a doubt. It can be rendered with, "Is it the case?"

15 I.A. Candrea and Ov. Densușianu, *Dicționarul Etimologic al Limbii Romîne: Elementele Latine* [*Etymological Dictionary of the Romanian Language: The Latin Elements*] (Bucharest: SOCEC, 1907).

16 All of these various expressions would be translated the same way in English, "either-or."

What about the interrogative *oare*? It is explained, the same dictionary says, by the primitive adverbial function as well (so still by the meaning of "now"). However, it seems more appropriate to say that the interrogative *oare* takes on itself the entire semantic evolution of the word, especially in the sense of the disjunctive. Indeed, doesn't the expression, "it is either one or another," move naturally into "is it one by chance, or is it another?"[17] All the general and indeterminate meanings that *ori* ("or") brings in composition — *oricând* ("anytime"), *oricare, orice* ("anything"), *oricum* ("anyhow") (or as a suffix, *alteori* ["other times"], *rareori* ["rarely"], *deseori* ["often"], *uneori* ["sometimes"]) — have solidarity with oare to the point of being replaced with it, so that one can say, *oarecum, oarecare, oarece* (with the original sense of "hour,"[18] and "time," *oară,* survives in expressions such as, *bunăoară* ["for example"], *odinioară* ["in times past"], *doară, deoarece* ["because"]).

In our language, the weaving of the interrogative with the disjunctive and with indetermination appears clearly from a second interrogative expression, an obsolete one, *au* (*au bate vântul?*[19]). *Au* is nothing else than the Latin *aut,* which could also have an interrogative meaning, but it has given only the correspondent of "or" in the other romance languages. In *Etymologicum magnum,* Haşdeu writes, "Only for Romanians did this conjunction develop the full interrogative meaning, so that it was specialized by it in comparison with the synonyms *sau* and *ori* = the old *veri,* and has come close to *ore,* the old *oare.*"[20] Just like *oare,* we add, this interrogative particle can give inde-

---

17 Noica emphasizes the semantic connection between the Romanian *ori* ("either," "or") and the Romanian *oare,* explained above. The two Romanian expressions translated here are, *ori e unul, ori e altul* and *oare e unul, oare e altul?*

18 "Hour" in Romanian is *oră.*

19 Similarly to *oare, au* suggests a doubt that is implied in the sentence: "is the wind blowing, per chance?"

20 Bogdan Petriceicu-Haşdeu, *Etymologicum magnum romaniae* (Bucharest: Editura Minerva, 1972), our translation. As in other places, Noica does not provide information about the page number or about the edition from which he cites.

terminate forms, even if they are rarer: *au-unde*[21] could be used in the Biblical translation in 1648. Indetermination and disjunctive opening are truly solidary with interrogation.

At the beginning of our inquiry, nothing seemed to take *being* under a question. In its expression, the question indicated a simple suspension of what is, by a simple raising of the intonation; then, the question gave an image of the inversion of things, as in a mirror, by inversion; finally, the question brought the pure and simple doubt about things to the point of denying them. But in this fourth way of forming itself, the question comes to show that it does not register the world as it is — at the most, the question suspends the world, by turning it upside down or denying it — but the question truly places the world in indecision as if the question were preparing new decisions in the world. And indeed, from forms with *va* — as in, *nu cumva* ("somehow"), *undeva* ("someplace"), *cândva* ("sometime") — one will be able to present this new and deeply characteristic work for a question, the work of opening toward a future world, with chances of tailoring paths in its indetermination.

5.

Out of the solidarity between disjunctive opening and interrogation, a new feature of the latter comes to surface, which indicates, this time, mature, reflective interrogation, that is, the indirect one. Direct interrogation, which too often has naivety, wonder, ignorance, or, at times, simulated ignorance, as well as doubt, uncertainty, and perplexity, does not render the complete measure of interrogativity; instead, it is its second modality ("is it a problem *if*..."). If disjunction is solidary with indetermination, this is because it represents its organization. From the way in which disjunction masters indetermination and organizes it in distinct parts of alternative, the question extracts, for its mature form, the term "*if*," which is so significant and

21 I.e., *Oare-unde?* "Where perchance?"

which, it seems, has such active functions in all languages. It can show, now, how much interrogation came out of any condition of ignorance; for "I don't know if..." or, "I don't know if it didn't perchance..." expresses precisely the contrary to ignorance.

"If" is not only hypothetical, but it is also thetic, that is, it institutes something. It is not only conditional and optative, but it is also deliberative. In a way, it reprises all the functions of a question: it suspends, mirrors, reverses, denies by its passing in unreality, affirms by indeterminate opening toward reality, and finally organizes indetermination. Grammar registers the fact that only total interrogatives are introduced by the conjunction "if." But it is natural to be so because the particular ones are organized from the beginning ("I wonder *who* is coming," "I want to know *how* it is"). Even more, as we could see, their interrogative particles are the expression of the categorial organization of things (i.e., when, where, how), and there is no more need of detachment from indetermination. At this step, a question means much more than ignorance or suspension and restraint when faced with something; it means taking hold of a domain, and this is so organized that, where the domain is not organized by the nature of the question, as in the case of a partial question, indirect interrogation comes to bring out the domain from its spread, gathering it under a condition, an assumption, and even a setting. Thus, when it goes into indirect modality, a question begins to affirm something, everywhere.

From unreality to necessary reality, the simple conjunction "if" (for us also *de*,[22] or some forms of inversion of the verb) traverses the spread of the zones that surround being. It accompanies the mode of the unreal ("if it were," "if it would have been"[23]) naturally, and it passes sovereignly through the affirmation of reality, which it modulates in various ways: "if it were

22 A shorter form for *dacă*, "if" in Romanian.

23 We are using the conditional perfect tense to express the Romanian future perfect tense. Since the English future perfect tense expresses an action that would have been completed by a certain time in the future, it doesn't capture the uncertainty suggested by the Romanian tense of the verb. We wanted to render that uncertainty by using the conditional.

not, it wouldn't be told," which is an indirect affirmation that it is; "if it was this way, it happened this way...," which is a temporal affirmation of what is; "if my time passes...," which is its causal affirmation; "if you don't want me...," it is concessive affirmation. It then reaches this expression, "if so... then," which belongs to Stoic and modern logics and leads to necessary inference, expressing the strongest necessity of situations and processes, their logical necessity. All of these, next to the dubitative, the potential, and the deliberative, are implied by the "if" of the indirect question, in which we see concentrated the entire nature of interrogativity that is described above.

However, once it passes into indirect modality, by which it comes out of spreading and begins to say something determined, doesn't interrogation prepare, perchance, its own extinction in answer?

This is where we see the function of question: it organizes, indeed, the indeterminate, together with the organization brought by categories, and it begins to say something, at the same time with "if" and with the alternatives in which it lays indetermination; it orients, it opens a horizon, and it regenerates reality. However, doing so, it shows a certain independence.

6.

Indeed, a question charges the world with possibility. It raises to life more than the answer can satisfies. In a sense, a question never covers itself, or it is never covered, by an answer; apart from the striking fact that any answer to questions of knowledge awakens in us questions or enlarges the old question (as it happened with modern science), the fact remains that the first question itself aroused a wealth of possibilities, which is maintained as an aura around the answer. The partial question, even that of existence — a simple question regardless of how immediate it was, a "who's coming?" — projects a fascicle of possibilities in the conscience of the questioner as well as on the thing questioned: many others could come other than the one who comes. By the simple fact of questioning, the world *has increased.*

We are now far from the auxiliary meaning of interrogativity, the meaning of being a simple method of investigation, information, specification, or control, in subordination to an answer. Not even the fact of being able to be a reply given to the world, in part and in whole, says everything about its essence. A reply is also subordinate to given situations, just as Plato's Idea was, when it seemed to double the world, while a question awakens new possible situations. Its possible remanent dwells in the essence of a question, and so the eventual novelty brought by it.

A question charges every situation with the novelty of the potencies which it projects over it; it so truly regenerates reality, not only in the sense of remaking it as it is, but also in the sense of redressing it. An electrical signal must be redressed when it is transmitted; otherwise it registers level falls. Interrogativity has this function of redressing: by it, the potential of reality is raised to a different level. When it is about thinking, such a function of redressing, possessed by interrogativity, appears as evident. But if one can talk about an interrogativity of things, then there still are level risings within them (any wave in the sea is an image of a question) by increasing the tension under which that thing finds itself and gets manifested.

Only now does a question justify its external expression from the bosom of speech. For why is a question made by raising the tonality? What is physical in this creation of disequilibrium or in this raising of level? A simple suspension, by which we justified it at the beginning, doesn't explain everything in the phonetic procedure of a question. Speech places the entire necessary load into a question in order to raise the potential or the tension of its content of thought and, in a way, of its content of reality.

Psychologically, just as a question goes through all the stages of the human realm, from the modest question of the one who is overwhelmed and ignorant to the certain question of the all-knowing one, the nature of a question also authorizes having a passage from the faded modality of its beginning to its current fullness.

With the possible worlds—and this in all the meanings of the possible, as we shall see—interrogativity brings an increased reality in the bosom of reality. Thinking has things to say about this increased reality, and, surprisingly, the infused thinking of our language or the Romanian philosophical sensibility speaks about it. It's true that all other approaches of a creating spirit also express this increased reality, or at least the possible of the world (mythical thinking as well as artistic thinking, for example, or in a rigorous fashion such as scientific thinking). However, only theoretical thinking is conscious of a new sense of reality and remains with it to the end.

A question is precisely that which prepares the access to such a supplemented reality, mobilizing the entire world of the spirit for this purpose, together with its various faculties. Sensibility, imagination, will, intellect, and reason take root, all of them, in the original approach of a question (the ancients spoke of "wonder"), which expresses the fact of the encounter with the external world and the opening toward its novelty.

When the spirit awakes in the world, it places the world under the sign of a question. Everything it sees is different than it seems at the beginning: it is a kind of a manifested cypher; it is law, meaning, and reason. But how is that which is possible?

II

Romanian Modulations of Being

When you see the seas, the rivers, and the springs, you naturally wonder: how is the sea possible? How are the rivers possible? But you do not wonder how the springs are possible, and even less the spring in general. You are overwhelmed by the immensity of the sea, as by the immensity of reality. Next to the passivity and placidity of the seas and oceans, you are surprised by the virtually undisrupted activity of the rivers (for the ancient Greeks, the rivers were masculine and the seas were feminine) just as, on the level of reality, the undisrupted processes from the bosom of this reality surprise you. The springs, however, remain in the infancy of nature.

However, the universe of the spring is more comprehensive, perhaps, than the universe of the sea, and in any case more complex. An ocean, in its apparent immensity, is still finite. In order for a spring with its undisrupted murmur to be possible, it's not only the unknown things from the depth of the mountains and earth that are needed, but the collaboration of the entire universe also. A more intimate and extensive solidarity than in the case of seas and rivers brings a simple spring into the world; to go deep into this world of creation is more difficult — but also filled with lessons — than to give an account about the great ponds and streams of water of nature.

This is at least what the modern man considered doing in culture. In general, on many deciding plans for culture, he no longer directly explored only the real, but also the possible. "In the past, the law was given by the existent; for us, it is given by the possible," a contemporary man of culture, the physicist Weizsäcker,[1] says. On the other hand, when he explores the real directly, he does it in order to see and get new possibilities, on the theoretical level as well as the practical one. He thus became a man with more possibilities than any other time, even compared with the man of Greek Antiquity, who served as a prototype for so long. He had more questions than him.

Surprisingly, Romanian-infused thinking did the same thing. Just like in the modern world, there is an investigation done by interrogativity in Romanian, which leads to an increase of the real in the bosom of reality. The implicit meditation on being that has been undertaken by the Romanian language throughout centuries deserves to be brought to light. It will prove to be that much more fitting as it will not come as a reprimand to the century, as in someone like Heidegger, but as an attempt of making everything full.

Since German thinkers believed that they can read so many things in the speech of their language and in the speech of Greek, there could be a justification for bringing to the game the experience of other languages. In Romanian speech, there is a large work of modulation of being. Why would it be less significant than the historical experience of other speeches? Thinking is faced now with a speech like ours in which we witness something that is strange at first sight and that doesn't take place in the same fashion in other languages: being, in its formulation as verb, "to be," can double itself, turn over itself, and combine with itself.[2] Doing so, it diversifies and enriches the idea of being.

Various linguistic formations can be obtained with the verb *a fi* ("to be"). Even if they don't really express "not to be," these

1 Carl Friedrich von Weizsäcker (1912–2007) is a German physicist and philosopher. Noica doesn't specify the exact source for the quote.

2 Noica refers to various verbal tenses in which the verb "to be" is used with different functions. He will explain these tenses in the following pages.

formations still speak about something else than "is." If you place yourself in the perspective of logic, you can see a good part of the so-called modal logic in them. Indeed, while "is" represents the affirmation of reality, for contingency, possibility, impossibility, or necessity, languages must usually put in place a special expression: "it happens," "it is possible," "it is impossible," "it is necessary." In Romanian, however, these modalities stem from the same "to be," which is composed with itself. *Ar fi să fie* ("it would be to be") expresses the possibility ("it is possible to be"); *n-a fost să fie* ("it was not to be") expresses impossibility, and *a fost să fie* ("it was to be") expresses necessity. *De-ar fi să fie* ("if it were to be") expresses something of the order of contingency with that "if," and this not in a subjective or deliberate sense, but in an objective sense — "if it happened to be."

If it is this way, it means that the modes of being spring from reality itself, or that the logic of the existent is the one that gives the logic of the possible and of the necessary. It's possible that some new aspects result from the perspective of the combination of "to be" with itself, and the first novelty would be that the modalities are more numerous than the classical five: possibility, impossibility, necessity, contingency, and of course, existence. Besides these, the modality of *va fi fiind* ("it may well be to be," the presumptive), the modality of *ar fi fost să fie* ("it would have been to be," the closed possibility), and a few others also appear.

It has been said that any adverb represents a modality, in a sense. In our use of the verb "to be" we have a criterium for restraining the modalities from the infinity of adverbial nuances: there wouldn't be an infinity of modalities, at least logical ones, but perhaps only those which the verb "to be" can give with itself. After all, this verb is the sovereign of the affirmations about being, including about the weakened, approximative, or at times strengthened forms of thought and speech in being.

This is how things are if you place yourself in the perspective of logic. If you move onto the perspective of being, then the experience of our language could give an even more interesting page. There is, of course, a perception of reality, be it total or partial, which we understand to qualify by "is." And there also is — outside of possible or necessary reality — a sort of imminence of real (*este să fie* ["it is to be"]), a tentative in the real (*era să fie* ["it was about to be"][3]), unfulfillments in the real (*n-a fost să fie* ["it was not to be"]), absolutizations in the real (*a fost să fie* ["it was to be"][4]), or relativizations in it. What regions of being do they describe? Isn't it about regions that are as significant as those we usually explore in "is"?

The expression *fragedă fire* ("tender nature"), sometimes used in our language's past by someone like Cantemir,[5] for example, is perhaps able to suggest the understanding of being that will be deciphered from its Romanian sentiment. *Fraged* stems, it seems, from the Latin *fracidus,* and the term is related to *frango,* which gives "fracture." A fusion between contraries, which is significant for the spirit and the creativity of our language, was produced here as well. The fracture, which is the disorder of the rigid, of the inert, of the inorganic, and of the bone, became solidary with tenderness, which belongs to the organic and the flesh. Incarnate in the real, entered in the time and the flesh of the real, being loses its rigidity. If it didn't, it would fracture by its simple incarnation into something else. It becomes tender, it

3 The meaning of this Romanian expression can be rendered in English only by using an adverb, "about," as we chose, or "almost," as it could also be rendered — "it almost was." We chose "it was about to be" because it maintains the double use of the verb "to be." In Romanian, this expression is formed by using the imperfect of "to be" to which you add the subjunctive.

4 This expression can render the Aristotelian *to ti en einai,* "that which it was to be." Here, it is not identical, because it doesn't refer strictly to the essence of a particular but rather to the general idea that something was destined to be. However, it is the same verbal expression that is used for translating Aristotle as well.

5 Dimitrie Cantemir (1673–1723) was a voivode of Moldavia, which formed, more than a century later, the state of Romania by its union with Walachia. Cantemir was also a man of letters. He is best known for his historical work, *Historia incrementorum atque decrementorum aulae othomanicae* [*The History of the Growth and Decay of the Ottoman Empire*]. His philosophical work is *Sacrosanctae scientiae indepingebilis imago* [*The Indescribable Image of the Sacred Science*], written in 1700 and known in Romanian under the title of *Metafizica* [*Metaphysics*] (Bucharest: Meditative Arts, 2017).

accedes to modulation, and it composes together with the world and with its momentary creations. Aren't all of them, the individuals, the thoughts, and the galaxies, momentary creatures in the great cosmos? Being, though, must be in them, and it can only do it by becoming tender, and not fracturing itself. Thus, seeing being in the world means walking on the footsteps of those situations in which being entered.

If you invoke the situations in which being places itself due to the forms of composition of the verb "to be" with itself, then you see that they can remind of the modes of the question, as they were to be found still in our language. There is thus a situation of suspension of being with "it would be to be," which can correspond perfectly to interrogative suspension. Then, there is one of reverse and of mirroring, just as in questions, with "it was to be." The negative of the question also appears in the situations of being, not only literally and directly with "it was not to be," but also indirectly with "it was about to be" (but it is not). Indetermination appears with "it may well be to be." Indirect question, using "if," seems rethought in those situations created by the same "it would be to be"; "it is to be" and "it was to be" (among those that could be) send the thought to disjunctive decisions and to the richness of alternatives found in the bosom of matured questions. The functions of a question are not foreign to the situations of being.

Broadly, Romanian speaking brings into play the following six situations of being, naming just as many regions from around the being that is present, which is of course the principle of life, the active factor of reality. It imposes itself in any language, and the originality of our language is to deploy some new modalities, which converge toward it and are validated by it:

N-a fost să fie ("It was not to be")

Era să fie ("It was about to be")[6]

---

6 This is a very difficult to translate expression. The problem stems from the fact that the imperfect of "to be" in Romanian can express both a past action and an almost accomplished action if you add a verb in subjunctive afterward. You may say, for example, *Era acasă când l-am vizitat* ("He was home when I visited him") and *Era să plece când l-am vizitat* ("He was

Va fi fiind ("It may well be to be")[7]
Ar fi să fie ("It would be to be")
Este să fie ("It is to be")
A fost să fie ("It was to be").

For all of these situations, being itself is the center, or rather the "point of accumulations," as in mathematics.

This is, then, the picture of the situations of being, in which the situation where being is reached, expressed by "is," appears to be absent but is in fact enriched.

1. *N-a fost să fie* ("It was not to be")

We can consider that the first ontological situation in the being conceived by our language — and perhaps the first situation of any thought about being (as of any *reality* of being, as we shall see) — is the one of "it was not to be." On first sight, it can seem surprising to say that the absence of being represents an ontological situation. Common users of Romanian, and thinkers within its horizon, understood erroneously this "it was not to be," as a sort of resignation of the mind and of the heart.[8] For the empty thought, a kind of modality of the impossible would appear here.

This is how things would look for the empty thought. But "it was not to be" must be understood; of course, it should not be justified by a value judgment but rather identified by a judgment of observation. If it is true that it expresses a situation that

almost leaving when I visited him," but he didn't leave). *Era să fie* implies the second expression here, so one could say, "it was almost being." We find this expression to be confusing in English, so we chose to translate it with "it was about to be" (but it didn't end up being).

7 The Romanian expression *va fi fiind* is realized by the future of the verb "to be" (*va fi*) plus its gerund (*fiind*). The expression suggests a presumption: "it is possible that it may be, but it is not certain." Or, "it has all the conditions to be, but we cannot know that it is or it isn't." In order to render this meaning, we added "may" and "well."

8 The "resignation" comes from the way in which the expression sounds in Romanian. One could interpret this meaning as "it was not *meant* to be."

stumbled upon the threshold of impossibility, something real still appears in its modality. That which "was not to be" *tried* to be; it knocked at the gate of reality toward to be, but it was not. The attempt *to be* cannot be foreign to the problem of being and it is not pure nothingness.

That which "was not to be" is not only interesting for mathematics because mathematics doesn't bring into play any domain of reality. Everywhere else, the *active* modality of the impossible, which is described in the analyzed formula in question, contributes to the edification of the real. For the physical real (for example, as for the human one in all of its manifestations), that which "was not to be" is precisely a situation in which being originates. The logical possible — that which is not contradicted — is lazy; the ontological one barely comes out of indifference by its passive orientation as virtuality. When Plato says that there is an immensity of nonbeing around any being, he gives expression to the thought that being has an aura, but one that is too vague. The nonbeing of each reality is not anything, as the ancient philosopher says, but one that is particular; similarly, the impossible of each reality is also one that is particular.

In the case of each natural reality, the scientific researcher, for example, explores also that which it *could not* be. In the tree of life, we are told, the world of insects could not reach a particular development of the cerebral life, as it happened with the mammals. Within every genus, species have tried their impossible. In dead nature and in living nature, all things that were not to be modeled those which are. In history, the fact that Spartacus's revolt did not succeed is not registered in the non-being of history but in its being.

How can we speak of an exclusive sense of submission, resignation, and fatalism in the recognition of those that were not to be? There is rather, or at least there was, a sense of knowledge and of large affirmation. As you go higher on the ladder of realities (in the regions of man, for example), that which was not but tried to be or that which proposed itself to being, is more clarifying for being. One cannot know the soul and the spiritual being of man without the impossibilities that he encountered. Historical life in a large sense, just as particular destinies, is delimited and modeled according with the reached and unsurmountable thresholds. The esthetic being itself or man's creations do not have sense and truth without the subtext of intentions and positive processes. Just as Michelangelo destroyed sculptures that did not belong to the esthetic nothingness, man's and society's life is rich in creative processes that are not objectified in works of art.

The state of being that is expressed by "it was not to be" is a clear modality in the service of being itself. For example, the fact that life on earth was produced based on carbon and that, in a sense, "it was not to be" based on silicon, is not only instructive on the scientific level, but also constructive on the ontological level. The fact that impossible things knock at the door of the real in nature and in the life of spirit makes out of these things a modality of being.

The first situation in which being can then be found is that of unfulfilled being. This fact was evidenced, for example, in the perspective that was opened by Marxism. History conceived on this basis brought to light social unrests and positive economical processes, which in their time, could not come out to light. They had an affirmative content of reality and were the anticipation of a full historical reality. In this presentation of being that our Romanian saying undertakes or at least suggests, this is followed by: suspended being ("it was about to be"), eventual and presumptive being ("it may be to be"), possible being ("it would be to be"), the being of entering into being ("it is to be," "it is about to be"), and the consumed being ("it was to be").

But the situations that this investigation brings to light prove to be modalities of being that, from now, seem also to say something else than what the direct investigation into being could bring to light. In any case, the traditional problematic of being has a regrettable tendency: wanting to catch the real, it actually gets more and more detached from it and tends to continually say that being is neither this, nor this; in the meantime, the Romanian modulation of being anchors itself more and more in the real and tends not only to say, "it is both this and this," but even to register the unfulfillments of being in the active of being.

The attempt to be is also a kind of being of reality, the kind of that which institutes itself. This is where being begins, with that which attempts to be. Everything that "was not to be" up to that which "was about to be" is thus inscribed in the being of the world.

2. *Era să fie* ("It was about to be")[9]

For the analysis of being, there is something suggestive in the difference between "it was not to be" and "it was about to be" (but it was not). With the first formula, which we analyzed above, being lacked something that belongs to the general. If a thing, a process, or a world, as an ensemble of things and processes, were not to be, this is because they lacked the group of general conditions that could make them possible — or rather, they could realize their potentiality — so because they had not reached their law, and they had not risen, despite the richness of their nature and manifestations, to that law which could consecrate, fix, and fulfill them.

On the contrary, the unfulfillment described by "it was almost to be" doesn't depend on the lack of something of the general, but on the lack of conditions of particular order, or the lack of individualization. A thing or a process "was to be," it had all the general conditions to be, but it was not due to a reason that seems accidental. It is not so much about a failure here but rather a suspension. The situation from "it was about to be" describes thus the suspended being.

9 We explained this formula when it first appeared in this volume (see chapter 2, n. 6). Here, we want to reiterate that this expression suggests that something — an entity or a situation — almost came into existence, but somehow it was not accomplished. Another possible rendering in English is, "it almost was," but this expression does not maintain the double use of the verb "to be."

Such a suspension appears fully in the bosom of reality, and it was signaled by Kleist,[10] with the philosophical spirit of all the romantics of high class (as the Germans or Eminescu for Romanians), who described this situation in the most penetrating way. Once while regarding a vault, he told himself that such a thing is possible precisely because the stone blocks of the vault tend to fall, and in their fall together they support one another, and they arch themselves. Thus, something "was about to fall" and did not fall because it was supported by something else, which also was about to fall. Their fall together was blocked.

Similarly, something "was about to be" and it ended up not being after all. If you think better about it, the entire inorganic, geological, and biological reality must be inscribed in such blocks and suspensions that dwell in the heart of existing things and even define them, just as the fall together determined, for that writer, the arching of the vault.

What are inhibitions for man if not states or processes that "were about to be" without being able to reach fulfillment? Freudian theory would only be about something that "is not" if we reserve only nonbeing for "it was about to be." And, beyond the limits of Freudism, which became itself a blockage of European culture, the entire spiritual reality of man, just as in the case of "it was to be," must wear in itself the presence and the traces of "it was about to be."

Intellectual thinking from the past did not manifest any interest for suspended being. You must find strange formulas such as "it was about to be" in languages like ours to be made attentive at the modalities of being beyond "it is." However, you inevitably encounter such modalities while you explore being because they are cyphered in the real, and the moment you want to give account for what can be called "being" of the real, you can no longer avoid them or pass them on account of nonbeing as you would do from the classical perspective of being.

Let us say then, following the romantic Kleist or the romantic Eminescu, that, from the perspective of Romanian language,

---

10 Heinrich von Kleist (1777–1811) was a German poet and writer.

being itself appears very non-classical since it can be found not only in the great edifices, but also in ruins.

The suspended being that we find in "it was about to be" — which the scientist surely encounters in so many cases and is even forced to often invoke it (biology must be filled with such suspensions) — appears strikingly in one of the most frequent human and social experiment, that of adversity. In those adversities that are never solved, so in the great tensions of the human real, there clearly is a blockage, and this in a positive sense, that is often reciprocal. However, it is interesting that even in the case of adversities that led to a result by the triumph of one of the parties, it can happen that the party that is historically active takes on itself the senses and the foundations of existence of the passive one. That which "was about to be" maintains a form of survival and a way of being in the being of the party that, in appearance, remained active alone. Just as it was said that the defeated educate their victors and just as Hegel[11] knew to show that the slave models his master, it can also be argued that a large part or even everything that "was about to be" in things and people contribute to edifying being.

A conception of being that leaves aside, in nonbeing, entire regions of the former, of the order of "it was about to be," becomes itself a conception about nonbeing. The Romanian view that we can get from its sayings, with their accumulated experience, maintains a more comprehensive meaning for being precisely because it expresses it in its unripe nature and in its apparitions in the bosom of reality.

11 Georg Wilhelm Friedrich Hegel (1770–1831) is one of the most important German philosophers. Noica's *Povestiri despre om* [*Stories about Man*] (1980) is an interpretation of Hegel's *Phänomenologie des Geistes* [*Phenomenology of the Spirit*] (1807). One of the accusations at Noica's political trial was that he was sharing "hostile" manuscripts, among which Hegel's work was listed.

3. *Va fi fiind* ("It may well be to be")

One can speak, then, of an unfulfilled being—that which "was not to be" and that which "was about to be." That much more we'll have to talk about being in the situations that follow, where there is neither unfulfillment nor blockage. Only with these situations, all of them together, can one explore being on its entire register. If these situations truly express being, then one can say of it, turning around one of Pascal's sayings: being is that whose periphery is everywhere and whose center is nowhere.[12]

Every thing that a thing "was not to be" and what it "was about to be" is inlaid in its being as impossible moments that it had to face and that approximated, limited, and modeled it in their way. (As far as he is concerned, man feels this fully when he reaches his thresholds; in the case of things, it happens the same way.) Just like this, "that which it may well be to be," eventual being,[13] is also inlaid in the being of a thing.

We can continue the exploration of being with the situation of "it may well be to be." Do we have now a situation of being as it is registered by conscience, so a situation of uncertainty and ignorance that thought has regarding being? Or is it again a situation of being itself as we'll try to show? What is then the status of "it may well be to be"?

From a grammatical point of view, the forms of this expression belong to that which was named the presumptive mode in the analysis of Romanian verbs. In some older books on grammar, it was called the potential mode. They express un-

12 Pascal's famous saying comes from his *Pensées*. He says in section 72, "The whole visible world is only an imperceptible atom in the ample bosom of nature. No idea approaches it. We may enlarge our conceptions beyond all imaginable space; we only produce atoms in comparison with the reality of things. It is an infinite sphere, the center of which is everywhere, the circumference nowhere."

13 "Eventual" being is a problematic translation, since the Romanian word *eventual* should rather be translated as "possible" in English. However, since Noica also uses "potential," we kept here the English term "eventual." It should be understood in the sense of potentiality.

certainty, perplexity, doubt, presupposition, probability (*ce o fi gândind* ["what would he be thinking"]), even concession with the conjunctive (*să tot fie* ["it may well be so"]), or an affective nuance with the conditional. But this mode is developed in our language as a separate conjugation. Linguist Elena Slave shows this in a remarkable study about the presumptive,[14] bringing to light the fact that the presumptive is a genuine conjugation because it brings into play time, mode (indicative, conditional, conjunctive), voice, person, number. Trying to explain how this presumptive could be formed, as it is composed of the verb "to be" and the gerund or the past participle of the respective verb, the author shows this aspect — totally interesting for how our ideas have worked in this space — that the Romanian language seems to have felt the need of its own form for the expression of doubtful actions.

At first, it seems, an older and less used form, such as the future II (*vei fi ajuns de mult* ["you must have arrived for a long time"][15]) received a nuance of presumptive. If this tense, which was a past in the future, maintained from the future aspect its uncertain character only and became a tense of the past for the presumptive, then, the ingenious author says, the future could be listed for the present tense; and if the perfect was composed with the past participle, the present could be formed with the present participle or with the gerund respectively (*o fi dormit*, "he may have slept" for the past, *o fi dormind*, "he may be sleeping" for the present). Once the indicative is obtained in two tenses, it was easy for the language to produce a conditional (*ar fi dormind*, "he would be sleeping") and a subjunctive (*să fi*

14 Elena Slave, "Prezumtivul" ["Presumptive"], in *Studii de gramatică* [*Studies in Grammar*], Vol. 2 (Bucharest, 1957).

15 Noica refers here to the tense future anterior, which designates an action that takes place in the future but anteriorly to another future action. In this case, the suggestion is that your arrival would take place sometime in the future but prior to another event taking place in the future. For example, "you must have arrived for a long time when I get there."

dormit[16]) because these are modes of doubt and of the possible par excellence. Language could even play, making doubt fall not on the verbal expression but on another part of the sentence (*ce o fi având cu mine?* ["*what* would he be having with me?"] where doubt falls on "what," while "would he be having" means effectively "has"[17]). Thus, the author [Elena Slave] concludes that from a single tense, which was the second future, we arrived at a mode, as presumptive is usually considered, but in reality, at a real conjugation. With such a conjugation, the Romanian language could express an experience that was particular to the language.

This is what happened in other languages as well but with other experiences and results of thinking. In Latin, the active future participle, also combined with "to be," just like our presumptive, gave a genuine conjugation, that is the active periphrastic, which expresses intention; the future passive participle gave the passive periphrastic, which expresses the obligation (*delenda est Carthago*).[18] One could add that in English, there is the conjugation with the gerund—just like in Romanian but with a different meaning—the so-called progressive conjugation, which expresses the concomitance, the co-presence of situations taking place. The Latins, thus, expressed *will* and *duty* by special conjugations, the Anglo-Saxons expressed precise *determination* of a situation or action, while our language expresses the *problematic*, the *possible*, the *presupposed* with an entire conjugation.

The spiritual experience that brought us to a new conjugation is, we dare say, somewhat more subtle than in the other two

16 In English, the infinitive or the past infinitive often takes place of the subjunctive, since it is usually a verb in a subordinate sentence that follows another verb. For example, one could say in Romanian, *Ar fi vrut să fi dormit* ("He would have like to have slept").

17 While the verb would normally suggest some doubt referring to whether someone has something with me or not, the construction of the sentence moves the doubt that is expressed through the verb to the pronoun: I know he has something with me, but I don't know what.

18 "Carthage must be destroyed," in Latin.

languages because it is not about intention, as for the Latins, nor is it about the simple states of fact as for the English; rather it is about *being itself,* especially when the presumptive is made inside the verb "to be."

Indeed, for man's conscience, being is not only a reality, but it also is an eventuality. Such a situation of being shows itself as essential to conscience, which not only understands to come out, but it also needs to come out of a given horizon in the heart of being. Everyone tells oneself, "A wise person may well be to be in me, but it hasn't come out yet." Every self-conscient being has its own isotopes. It thinks of the world in the same way. "There may well be to be something else as well," a being tells itself; and it can say it in gradation, starting from the simple indifference and detached objectivity ("something may well be to be there, but I'm not interested"), to the intensity and dramatism of conviction ("something may well be to be there, which interests me directly").[19]

Any creator addresses a witness or a spectator, at least in a presumptive way. Creation has no meaning without the presupposition of someone who would understand it, use it, and assume it in the sense that the creator dreamed; not only the creator of art, but also any producer of goods, values, or meanings, needs eventual being (the presumed buyer, at least, for the producer). On the other hand, in its exercise of knowledge, as in the moral or emotional experience, conscience cannot presuppose other realities besides those that are given to it directly, other and better consciences that rebuke it or vibrate in consonance with it.

At the scale of humanity, the same experience of the presumptive took place in its passing from indifference to troubling certainty. There have been many centuries since scientists showed that the earth is only a planet and that there "may well be to be" other rational beings in the wideness of the cosmos.

19 We used "it may well be to be" for the entire paragraph, even if it sounds exaggerated in English. Of course, one may render that as "it might be," but we wanted to maintain the doubling of the verb "to be."

For a long time, this presupposition has not changed anything in the notion about man. Just as an individual can presuppose the existence of thousands and thousands of persons without having contact with them and can live as if they didn't exist, speculative thinking has spoken of reason as if it appeared in its human version only.

In fact, we will remain in this condition until an eventual contact with other rational beings; but today's certitude that "may well be to be for sure" such beings came to show the exceptional condition of man, who attempts to explain things and life according to a model. The conscience of such a situation is destined, now, to change something in the science about man; far from paralyzing it, this conscience will bring into play the presumptive in order to investigate, with or without direct contact, the possible isotopes of rational being.

However, the theme of isotopes brings back before us the things themselves. In everything said above, with the presumptive, it was about a situation of being as it is registered by conscience. Doesn't "it may well be to be" render, though, a situation of being itself? The eventual, the suspension, the probability, a kind of uncertainty, and even a doubt as *în-doire*[20] can have an objective meaning. If you are making a metaphor by saying, "nature wonders," when you say, "nature bends itself/doubts,"[21] it doubles itself, and you express a reality that conscience had to register with surprise at the same time with the fact of isotopic from the bosom of chemistry.

Indeed, nothing in the hypotheses that led to the scientific experiment authorized the idea of a multiplied being. Formal logic, either traditional or new, prohibits it formally with a principle of identity and of non-contradiction that does not allow for a thing to be something else and someone else than itself. Without the identity of things, their knowledge didn't seem possible.

---

20 See chapter 1, n. 5 about doubt and *în-doire*.

21 The same *în-doire*.

However, things themselves came to show that they have a different kind of identity. Knowledge must then change its principles. Elements (oxygen, for example), just like substances (water, for example) have isotopes which, physically, are the same since they only differ due to neutrons; chemically, they occupy the same place in the table of elements or in the inventory of substances, even if they have different atomic weights or properties. On top of the fact that there are isotopes in some cases, the majority of elements are a mixture of isotopes. This represents a novelty in the heart of the conception about material beings. In the case of man, before the phenomenon of isotopy, one could speak at most about an associated being as it happens with the heroes whose destinies are indissolubly interwoven (Castor and Pollux, for example); but only now did reality bring to life a plural being, a mixture under the image of a unitary being.

Being itself, as individual reality at least, thus doubles itself, or it multiplies. Next to what it is in immediacy, being will possibly be, or it may well be to be something else as well. Being *is* as *being-something-else* also. Suspended in its isotope versions, doubled, and multiplied three or five times, being is one in a different way.

You don't have, then, access to being only by "it is," which, even if dominating, can have around it a whole constellation. You must see also what a real existence "may well be to be" in order to have access to its complete being. Being can be understood only in its own spreading or as brought together and remade out of its own diversity. With a suspended, eventual, or probable being, so with the experience of reality rendered by "it may well be to be," a new chapter in the phenomenology of being is written based on the Romanian modulations of "to be."

4. *Ar fi să fie* ("It would be to be")[22]

If "it may well be to be" describes a somewhat exterior region of being, even when it is about its own isotopes, "it would be to be" brings into play both something engaged and something detached that knock at the doors of reality.

It is not, but neither is it foreign to being. It would be to be. It has all the elements to be, and the next thing would be to be. Perhaps it is even at this moment, but this is not what is interesting. Rather, it is its justification to be. Or perhaps it is not, but nothing prohibits it from being. "It would be to be" is on the steps of being, and it sniffs it out (with an exact word, which became inexactitude itself when it expresses approximation as sniffing something), just like all Romanian modulations of being do as they are placed either before or after being.

That which is between "to not be" and "to be" has proven, in a sense, more significant than nonbeing and being in their fixation. Just as our power our creation cannot say directly something essential about a hero but must "narrate" him, reason cannot give account about being without depicting its phenomena and states, so without doing its phenomenology. Our language undertakes such a phenomenology about being.

Thus, we must say again, with every situation that we invoke: "it is" by itself does not express the entire being because it does not give an answer to the question that it itself is asking: what is in things or in the world? To answer "what is" you must also see — with the above modalities of the Romanian language — everything that was not to be, was about to be, may well be to be, together now with what would be to be.

There is an ascending pursuit of being in all of this. "It was not to be" maintains, in its negative, something from "to be not"; "it was to be" forgets the negative but falls back into it at the end;

---

22 This phrase may also be translated with, "it is about to be." The similarity with the other expression, "it was about to be," is important. It the former one, something almost was, but it ended up not being. In this situation, something is about to be, and nothing stops it from being.

"it may well be to be" brings forward the presupposed possibility of being, while "it would be to be" brings its assured possibility and thus a beginning of founding it.

If "it would be to be" expresses the possible, then it must be said that, in a way, the possible spreads also over the other described situations: unfulfilled being, suspended being, and eventual being. Although they were present in being, these three represented a form of possible from before the possible, and they came to give, in their beautiful formula in the Romanian language, depth and past to a possible that seems to be the past of the real. However, even if they precede the possible, these situations truly belong to being and say something essential about it, as they describe its limits on the one hand and its eventualities on the other. What would remain from being without its limits and without its eventualities, which give it not only its fairy-like character, but also its more exact image, its isotopes?

Described in its limits first then by its eventual, being can be now followed by its possible or its possibles. Usually, however, "possible" says too little. The paradox of the possible is that, being related with *posse* and in final instance with *potentia,*[23] it is deprived of any power. It expresses even the lack of power, in a sense. If it does not represent a form of indifference ("it can be, but it can also not be"), it wears in it a passivity that condemns it to inertia, regardless of the plan in which it may appear. Leibniz's possibles remained lazy in the divine intellect, until the intellect decided to choose and accomplish the least imperfect one. The possibles would only be the reserve fund of the world and not something in its reality or actuality.

With "it would be to be," though, we can recover the understanding of the possibles. Even if this expression is at its lower limit a "simple possibility," it is an oriented one. At any step, it has in itself the appetite of being and expresses a reference to the real, not a withdrawal from it. It does not contradict itself (which represents the "logical possible") and it does not contradict the real (which represents the "physical possible"), but it

23 Latin in the original.

also proposes itself to being, without waiting for external conditions to realize itself, as the usual possible does. It is a possible with self powers, a potentiality. If it doesn't succeed to be, it is because an impotence came from it and not from the things that oppose its realization. The entire being, then, in one of its situations, is that which "would be being." This is because "to be" is also "to not be yet."

Usually, the possible has been opposed, in academic terms, first to the impossible, second to the necessary or, third to the real. But all three oppositions fall in the version of "it would be to be." To not be real yet, for example, doesn't mean at all the refusal of the real; on the other hand, having the necessary reference to the real means not opposing necessity either. As for the first opposition, that between possible and impossible, it can be left to the simple exterior expression. On the contrary, now, under the suggestion of the situations of being in Romanian saying, it could be said that even the impossibility from "it was not to be" represented an unaccomplished possibility and not a pure and simple impossibility. Only the possible takes then the image of impossibility, as it also takes the image of necessity. It does not oppose them, as it opposes the real.

Those thinkers who do not understand remaining in modal logic see this final sense of the possible, that of not contradicting the real. In a simple article of an *Encyclopedia,* a thinker from last century Émile Boirac[24] has this profound thought, that the possible is not "pure nothingness"; it has definite properties, affinities, and repugnancies, in a word a nature "as if it existed." Regarding another author, who defined the possible as that which has all conditions to be apart from one, Boirac notices that if that unique condition is definitively absent, then the possible is transformed into impossible.

We shall not say that the formulas in our language resolve any problems raised by possible being, but, although our language brings up new problems, it also places the theme of the possible in a perfectly rational order. This is because a reason of

24 Émile Boirac (1851–1917) is a French philosopher and writer.

our language, which is less rigid than the one of the formal logician, comes now to show with "it would be to be" three things that are ignored by the possible of the logician.[25]

First, "it would be to be" gives to the possible a status of autonomy. Usually, as the simple possible, it is so little autonomous that an ancient philosopher affirmed that only the real justified the possible, or that, only as long as a thing is, it could also be — as one were to declare that the sun can move since it is moving. If it was not absorbed in the real at other times, the possible was polarized by it as an antonym (the seed, for example, which has an independent reality), or as imagined realities in who knows what divine intellect. Otherwise, only the real would be that which justifies and sustains everything.

However, the possible justifies itself in the Romanian formula. You will no longer be able to say, "since the sun is in motion, it would be to be in motion." In its new version, the possible effectively receives a status of autonomy. In a sense, "it" is even that which justifies the status quo, and often you "distance" yourself from the real in order to see how it was possible, so in order to give it a foundation. Even the one who accepts being as a given analyzes it and so decomposes it into its elements and functions; this person does nothing else than go in the opposite direction, from that "which is" to that "which would be to be."

This is because, second, "it would be to be" suggests the justification and thus the law of those that are. The ordinary possible seems to be only a schema, and when we deal with the logical possible ("that which can be thought without contradiction") no prefiguration of the real has place in it. On the contrary, if a thing would be to be, it means that it has long exceeded the exigence of not having an inner contradiction and that it prefigures the real more than an ideal schema. But now the idealist reversal is not produced. In the language that brings to play a formula

25 This is a difficult sentence to translate, primarily because the agents are two inanimate things: the language and the possible. Noica states that the possible ignores these three "things" that the Romanian language reveals in the expression "it would be to be."

such as "it would be to be," being itself is the one that affirms its essential image, and the reason of god or of man does not come to prescribe it.

With "it would be to be," our language thus says a third thing, that the idea of a logical possible leaves in the shadow. With the possible, a concentration must take place, and this concentration is not found in the loose use of the word (as in "anything is possible"), in the careless speaking or thinking. After being in limitation, with "it was not to be" and with "it was about to be," being is now concentrated around something that "would be to be." It is like a circle that tightens.

In the description of being that is described in our language, being is thus followed step by step as if it were an organized approach. With the next step, with "it is to be," the concentration will be more accentuated, as if our language showed how the genesis of being is possible in its discourse about it.

5. *Este să fie* ("It is to be")

"The world has more genius than me," Goethe used to say. It can be added that the wisdom of the world knows deeper things than the wisdom of a language alone can say. But every language is, after all, the wisdom of the world in one of its versions. This wisdom of the world needs the particular wisdom of language in order to explore reality in all the ways and to transfer its knowledge into words. From such words and specific turnings of phrase, the wisdom of the world requires accountability regarding the investigations that were done in its name.

It has been affirmed many times: being *is*. Our Romanian thought says not only "it is," but also "it is to be." What can there be in this curious turning of phrase? What exploration of being is registered in it?

It is clear that "is" cannot mean "exists" in this formula; it makes no sense to say, "it exists to be." On the other hand, the verb "to be" is neither used here as a simple auxiliary. It has the full meaning—and it could be said that it forms—with "is," a real sentence. You can better see the meaning in a formula with another verb than with "to be" itself (for example, "it is to rain"). Here, it could mean "it is on the verge of,"; "it follows to"; "the conditions are given for the thing"; or purely and simply, "it *must* rain." In this use, the verb of existence takes on a sense of necessity, even if a weak one.

However, the regime of obligation brought by "is" is nuanced, as it can be seen in the conditional formula. Indeed, you can say, "if it is to rain," "if it is to be," and this formula is in fact the most often encountered, as it is seen in "if it is to happen this way, then..." Here, "is" expresses clearly "is going to be" in such a way that it gives the impression that it expresses a simple future. In the *Dictionary of the Academy*, a quote from Varlaam[26] is given, which sounds this way: "If our bodies *iaste să hie*[27] more beautiful than the flowers of the field after the resurrection of the dead..." The linguist places the translation for *iaste să hie* in parenthesis: ("if they will be").

Is there a simple nuance of the future in the suspension brought here by "it is" followed by another verb? It is more than that, even in the formula of the conditional. "If it is for our bodies to be more beautiful" means for us: "if our bodies are *meant* to be more beautiful"; "if it is given to them"; "if indeed this is their law." And now, returning to the unconditional use of the expression "it is to be," we see well that this is its meaning. "It is to be," which means it is ordained, meant, given necessarily, and decided to be.

Who decides? The law of the thing, respectively the law of being, which is invoked by our language's entire exploration into being, as we have suggested. Being dwells under a law, or rather

26 Most likely, Noica refers to Varlaam Moţoc, Metropolitan of Moldova between 1632 and 1653, and editor of *Carte Românească de Învăţătură* [*Romanian Book of Learning*] in 1643, also known as *Cazania lui Varlaam*.

27 Archaic language, *este să fie*, which we've translated as "it is to be." In English, "If our bodies are to be more beautiful...." In order to maintain the expression "it is to be," one could also say, "If it is for our bodies to be more beautiful...." See also the suggestion of the future in the translation offered at the end of the paragraph, "it will be."

being has grounds.[28] Perhaps man's thinking has not held being accountable in all languages. Here, though, with this return and reflection of "to be" over itself that our language brings forward, with its reduplications, being seems to search for its own grounds.

"It was not to be" showed that a thing has not reached its law; it was neither an empty impotence nor something foreign from the manifestations of being; it brought them into play and tried, with the entire pre-being present in it, to bring itself into being,[29] but its grounds weren't the genuine grounds of being, and being did not receive it in its bosom. On the contrary, "it was about to be" wore in it the law and thus had all the reasons to be, but something accidental, as if coming from the outside, blocked it. "It may well be to be" then appeared to express the promise of being precisely in the measure that its grounds were in play; this is because the situation expressed by "it may well be to be" cannot be thought without the justification of "to be," a justification that is not exhausted by that which actually is but rather allows itself to be spread in all the richness of that which can be.

"It would be to be" came, on its turn, to concentrate the justification to be around a reality that had a law indicated by "it would be to be." Here, it was no longer about a possible that floats freely in the ocean of reality, as the possible from "it may well be to be" was but rather a possible concentrated on its law and thus justified to be. However, "it would be to be" invoked the law *prior* to the being of a thing. Only "it was to be" will invoke the law from *after* the consummation in reality of that

---

28 We translated the Romanian term, *temeiuri*, as "grounds." Other possible translations would be "reasons" or "foundations." Temeiuri comprehends the meanings of all of these terms. The "grounds" of something should be understood as being its support, its reasons of being, and also its final cause of being, in an Aristotelian sense.

29 "Bring itself into being" renders the Romanian reflexive verb *a se înființa*. The verb *înființa* brings together the preposition "in" and the noun *ființă*, "being." When the verb is not reflexive and is used in its transitive form, so only *a înființa*, it expresses the action of establishing or starting something, of placing the grounds for that thing, as in the example, "John and Mary have established a foundation."

thing. Isn't there any instance in the interval between them? This instance is precisely the step of "it is to be," which brings concentration on the grounds of a being until its imminent crossing into reality. With "it is to be" we have the situation of being as *entrance* into being.

This discourse about being—which goes so naturally from limitation to suspension, then to expansion, to concentration, and now to condescension and sedimentation of being—was possible because, after all, the idea of being is rational, in the implicit conception of the Romanian language.

It may seem odd to revindicate rationality for a language created by the ordinary people, at least in its first stage of development; however, if a linguist as the American Lee Whorf[30] could say that the language Hopi of Native Americans[31] was, in many aspects, more appropriate for the theory of relativity than German or English, we will not be shy about believing that a language with noble origin and impressive development such as Romanian has something to say to reason.

The idea of being was not always invoked rationally; being has not shown its "grounds," we will say using the terms of our language. It appeared rather as intuition or as an indisputable, evident, and overwhelming given. Thus, anyone who invoked divinity as ultimate being has passed openly beyond the limits of reason with such an idea of being. But even on the line of philosophical atheism, being could be non-rational. The unique substance of Spinoza,[32] the "Nature" which is cause for itself, while it does not allow for the existence of any substance in the world, it has no grounds[33]—it proclaims itself. It is a kind of,

30 Benjamin Lee Whorf (1897–1941), US linguist. His idea that languages shape how their speakers perceive and conceptualize the world is certainly important for Noica's own discussion about how the Romanian language conceptualizes reality.

31 Noica uses the term *pieile roșii* ("Redskins"). The text was written in a century and culture that had no connection with discussions regarding the offensiveness of this term.

32 Baruch Spinoza (1632–1677), Dutch philosopher.

33 The verb *a se întemeia* has as root the noun *temei,* which we previously translated as ground. Another possible translation here is "it doesn't get

"I am who I am." For Hegel, being, the Spirit, proposes itself massively and absolutely, and its dialectical rolling explicates it rather than justifies it. It also is that which it is, respectively that which it becomes.

There's something ruthless for reason in almost all traditional, that is, pre-Marxist, views on being. When it is not searched in its core and considered untouchable, it is intuited in its undisputed massiveness. Romanian being, on the contrary, as it is encrusted in the experience of the language, is gentler, more accessible, and more rational. It does not appear as an absolute center that would be present everywhere and would have a circumference that is nowhere to be found; it appears, on the contrary as we were saying as a circumference that is everywhere, while its center is nowhere to be found. It is a being that takes being, every time, and, precisely because of this, a being that appears as less ruthless with thinking since it has been itself tried together with everything that is through it.

In fact, not everything that "is" indeed has being in this view of ours. That which is can also be passing, episodic, and thus *neființător*,[34] we say. But if "it is to be," it means it has a law.

The problem of being, then, is, in ultimate instance, its law, which reason requires in any of the situations in which it is engaged. In this sense, every situation or level of being described above has more ontological significance, or, in any case, more expressivity, than the simple intuition and affirmation of being. In particular, "it is to be" says, in a way, more than "it is" because it invokes the reason to be.

Of course, a simple formula — after all, the law is reduced to what is established and to what must be — cannot replace an organized ontological exam. Such an exam can be imagined on the line of these formulas, which are just as many ways to explore the rationality of being.

---

established" or "it is not justified."

34 *Ființător* is the noun formed from the verb *a fi*, "to be," which expresses the one who has the quality of being engaged in being. *Neființător* is the one who does not have this quality, or, one may say, the one that participates in nonbeing.

It is true that, in this way, we do not speak of the great being of the world but of the being of particular things and states. It seems, however, that even in this context our language has a modern character, sending us not to being but to fields of being, just as in the modern scientific vision there is no longer talk about space but about spatial fields. When we ask, though, "what remains for the great being of the world?" we will answer that our language was not unaware of this problem. If it did not respond in this case as well with a full "it is," this is because it prepared a different, more rational answer — "it was to be"; and, as we shall see at the end, it became *întru* that which was.

6. *A fost să fie* ("It was to be")

According to some logicians, there would no place for anything between "is" and "is not." Everything would take place just as it does for mechanisms — it is, or it is not; it is open, or it is closed; the current passes, or it does not. There is a great truth here. Its applications, with cybernetics, may either make the world happy or not, according to the worries of Norbert Wiener.[35] However, if there is nothing between "is" and "is not," the Romanian language changes the way of talking and saying with almost equal strength: "it was not to be" and "it was to be." Between these two, there is something despite what some of the logicians say.

In this case, between "it was not to be" and "it was to be" there are some situations of being that, together with these two, give a more orchestrated image about being. Being is no longer understood as an overwhelming presence, since it is at times found in modalities such as, "it may well be to be," "it would be to be," and "it is to be." Being has a foundation this time.

In fact, the question about being — more precisely, which is the *true* being of this thing? Which is the true being of the world? — does not require an immediate presence, but it is precisely the coming out of presences, in order to establish which

35 Norbert Wiener (1894–1964), US mathematician and philosopher.

is the true being. The periphrastic Romanian formulas formed with the verb "to be," or, respectively, the spiritual experience regarding being that is registered in our language, says something about this second being.

At a first sight, or in any case, at a shallow look, our spiritual experience seemed to some, as we mentioned, one of resignation. "It was not to be," you tell yourself, and you seem to accept it as a fatality; or, "it was to be," and you accept it as something prescribed, as a "this is how it was written." At a second look, though, things seem different, and our experience about being proves to be a rational one. If it is not the experience of a formal reason, it is one that searches for grounds and pries the real in this direction, and so a rational search that represents the contrary to a resignation and submission or consent. In the light of these situations that are comprised in between the two extremes, between "it was not to be" and "it was to be," they themselves appear to be something else than what they seemed to be. For if it was about the search for the grounds of being, then "as it was written" does not have a fatalist meaning. If you say "written," you also say, "read."

Being has a code that can be read or not, just as it can be accomplished or not. There are, of course, many things of which it can be said that they are "in being," but still that being is not in them, in the sense that they do not accomplish its code or its law in them and with them. Similarly, there can be many spiritual expressions of being, but they may not give the grounds of being, so they do not read well in its code. With every step, beginning with "it was not to be," which was to be understood as an attempt to be with a minimum ground in the bosom of being, our meditation about being has concentrated the investigation around a foundation[36] to which we can tell the law of being just as the medieval were telling it its essence.

In simple terms, if "being" means both essence and existence — as its meaning is consecrated in general use, a meaning out of which we can no longer come — then the Romanian spir-

36 We preferred to use "foundation" instead of "ground" here.

itual experience about being is one in its essence. When, faced with fulfilled being, you say, "it was to be," then you no longer refer to the existence of the thing; you refer to its essence, to its law of being. Here, we unexpectedly encounter the German language, which seems to have made the term for essence, *Wesen,* from "what it was," *gewesen,* in the sense that, for German as well, a thing is truly what it was to be.

All things are now shown by this final situation, of consecrating being, represented by "it was to be." The limits of being, its eventuality, its possibility, and its imminence are confirmed, as it was natural, by its fulfillment. This means that the entire painting of being allows itself to be unfolded under the sign of "what is not yet" together with "what is no longer." Just as one cannot consider that the present tense has a form of consistency (it is a simple passing, it's been affirmed, and if you say "now," it has already passed, so it is no longer a now), the present of being or the present being does not unfold all of its grounds to be. The grounds to be are also given indirectly by the unfulfilled or suspended being and directly by the eventual being, the possible being, the being of the entrance into being, and, finally, the fulfilled being.

Essence expresses this character of fulfilment. Precisely due to this, essence is not the simple possibility from prior to the real, but the possibility from after it; it does not say what a thing remains to be but rather what it has truly become. However, even if it expresses something in the order of essence, "it was to be" doesn't close the problem of being either. On the contrary, it can be said that it decidedly opens toward it. Meaningfully, this new opening takes place this time toward the past.

Until now, all the situations of being opened toward being as if toward a future thing: they approximated it with "it was not to be" and "it was about to be," presupposed it with "it may well be to be," prepared it with "it would be to be," and announced its apparition with "it is to be." They all belonged to pre-being in the literal sense of the word, as being prior to being. Now, with "it was to be," the opening is done toward the past as well as toward the future.

Thus, far from being an epitaph for reality, "it was to be" represents the situation in which the grounds for being can be considered. These grounds are the significant ones, if being is not a simple presence but a foundation.[37] Their investigation was, after all, clearly reclaimed by modern thinking. In the bosom of the latter the question of "how is a thing possible?" and with Kant, "how was a thing possible?" appeared.

You can then take the Romanian formula as an expression of fatalism only if you don't want to go deeper; but when you prolong its meaning to organized analysis, you are authorized to bring it close to modern investigation, which is a critical approach so exactly opposite to fatalism. There is a certain exigence of rationality in both, and this at least authorizes a coming together of what is Romanian and what is modern.

If the investigation on our language on being says that being possesses a reason to be, a code, a structure, grounds, which are they? Our experience in being binds us to this, and not to abandonment, under the pretext that we would be faced with a simple resigned popular wisdom.

"To be, sad and empty folly, / Your ear lies to you and your eye deceives you," our poet said.[38] But it remains to be seen how much he is ours and how much he is himself when he says this; doesn't he perhaps become the echo of his great readings? Such words seem to be rather destined to people with a too rigid, logical conscience, spirits that have reached Hamletian monologues on the theme of "to be or not to be," as if these two together would not belong to a spiritual experience of being. Those who dwell, on the contrary, at the antipode of a rigid, logical conscience, the spirits that consent to nothingness and dissolution, as one would find in certain currents of Indian culture, are also meant to speak the same way. For them, "to be" is indeed a sad and empty folly since everything is illusion on a background of nothingness.

37 Noica using the same term, *întemeiere*, mentioned above,

38 Mihai Eminescu, "Mortua est."

Things are different for us, and Eminescu himself will prove it despite his poetical sadness that is, at times, formulated in other people's terms which he transfigured esthetically. "To be" has steps that begin from the rumor of being, go through the ascending preparation of being that is about to appear, and end in the fulfilled being. But we do not say only "it is" even for fulfilled and accomplished[39] being. We also say, "it was to be," understanding that the law of the thing has been revealed, as a written text.

If we understand by "written" the variety of prescriptions,[40] we will encounter the Romanian sentiment of being; if we understand purely and simply "written," then we'll have to read the text, and so attempt the possible rational deciphering of the text and of the texture of being.

---

39 The Romanian term used here, *săvârșit,* has the meaning of having been already accomplished, something that has reached that what it was supposed to reach from its conception.

40 Pre-writings in the sense of writings that have been already done prior to their accomplishments.

III

The Sentiment of Being

Whoever has before him the picture of the modulations of being can no longer do the injustice of considering the Romanian soul to have a singular tonality, the one of *Miorița*.[1] This ballade may be a unique accomplishment of our folkloric creation, but it is not also the unique measure for the philosophical sensibility of a soul that perceives *to be* and *not to be* inexpressibly better orchestrated.

There are several ways of being, respectively of nonbeing, for the Romanian soul. The injustice that the Romanian understanding of being has suffered due to the fact that people have dwelt too much and unilaterally on *Miorița* is just like the too brief philosophical attempts usually done about our word *dor*.[2]

---

1 *Miorița* is a Romanian ballade, considered by some to express the Romanian soul. In it, one shepherd is betrayed by his brothers and has a monologue addressed to one of his sheep. The poetry is a continued lament of someone who makes peace with what he considers to be his destiny prior to the fulfillment of this destiny. *Miorița* is the poem of resignation but a resignation stemming from a communion with the universe. As Noica mentions further, the Romanian philosopher who fully engaged the sentiment of the *Miorița* is Lucian Blaga.

2 *Dor* is a word that many consider untranslatable. Bishop Bartolomeu Anania said about *dor*: "*Dor* has always a purpose, a direction; it goes somewhere. [...] You have *dor* for someone you had and you lost, or for someone who is far away. [...] The *dor* attracts you, it attempts to fill a spiritual emptiness, and it is always expressed ineffably, so it cannot be

(We want to clarify that the reservations expressed here do not regard the thought of Lucian Blaga, who has accomplished his philosophy of culture and not the philosophy of being, under the sign of the *mioritic*.[3]) The functions and the suggestions of the word *dor* are indeed of first order, and we revealed them in a work about Romanian words, where we retained especially two functions: first, the semantic one, in order to prove that rational harmony is accomplished in our language between opposites (pain and pleasure, in the case of *dor*), by the fusion of meanings and not by composition; the second function, the philosophical one, in order to suggest that there is a field, a summary, a horizon around any concept, and this can occasion even a theory of the fields of knowledge and of logic. In its content, though, the word *dor* is too loaded with sentimentalism, so that speaking about a type of thinking by *dor* means making philosophical romanticism. Similarly, attempting to render the Romanian conception of being by *Miorița* means limiting yourself to a singular sound; otherwise, you would need to force the limits of an admirable poetical piece which cannot say more than what a ballade can say.

In general, you cannot explore the sensibility of a community or its conception about life and being by looking into only one vocable, such as *dor*, or even a singular popular or educated poem. How would the conception of life of the English people look like if it were drafted on the basis of a sonnet or even on the basis of Shakespeare's admirable collection of sonnets? Of course, some characteristic aspect of the English spirit would come to surface, namely the life of high society with its refinement of feeling and thinking; but the sentiment of the caducity of all things before the "devouring time" would also come to surface, the sentiment of which the *Sonnets* speak, as the only

placed into words." We think the best rendering into English is "longing." We have heard these words in a recording of a homily on the Sunday of the Prodigal Son.

3 The second volume of Lucian Blaga's *Trilogia culturii* [*The Trilogy of Culture*] is titled *Spațiul Mioritic* [*The Mioritic Space*] (Bucharest: Cartea Românească, 1936).

reply before this irremediable caducity, literary creation, and, largely, art; but these things are no longer characterizing Shakespeare's community. For the Anglo-Saxons have not brought to the game the ethos of great sorrows nor that of creations in pure, non-utilitarian, non-practical, and a-historic spirit, but rather they have brought the affirmations and the realizations of a different order, such as the parliamentary life and individual freedoms, empiricism, machinism, industrialism, and mathematical logic.

The conception about life and being of a world truly belongs to a world. You must search for the world's intimate meanings in its vastness; and if it were imputed to us that, at least for now, we have searched for the conception about being of the Romanian world in language only and in some specific forms of speaking, we would reply: a language expresses the vastness of a community. Even if we were to restrain ourselves to that which we have obtained thus far, we would be able to say that, unexpectedly, perhaps, the conception about being of the Romanian world is infinitely less simplified than the academic, traditional, and modern ontologies, and perhaps this is why its lesson deserves to be retained philosophically or pre-philosophically.

In its appearance so far, the idea of being proved more complex and perhaps, in a good sense, more intricate than in the traditional theoretical views. Why would *being* be monolithic? In the thought of Chesarie Rîmniceanul,[4] the great scholar and exceptional writer of Romanian language at the end of eighteenth century (so from the mature hour of our language, before it entered in contact with the modern and related languages), there is something about pre-being and being when he says in his and his time's terms: "Divine providence, running with steps without noise and voice without hearing, says... to one to hide, to the other to appear." Perhaps this is what being does, as we have seen it in its modulations: in a place, it is hidden, in anoth-

4 Chesarie Rîmniceanul (?–1780), Romanian scholar and bishop of Rîmnic. His interest in the origins of the Romanian people was certainly important for Noica's work.

er it is about to appear, and in others, it is fully shown. Chesarie's thought above is in fact followed by something even more characteristic to being, as it can be read in the *Menaion*[5] for January.[6]

Writing about the dominions that succeeded in Wallachia, Chesarie says indeed words of a rare insight on any plan, including the one of ontology. He writes, "The rule of Wallachia, being even more submitted to the unstable law of human things, having its flow through ravines and hidden stones, having its shores without havens, was similar to the *paliries* (from *paliroia,* which means "reflux" in Greek[7]), and so with the waters that run upwards in the morning, until a certain time when they flow downwards."

Under the suggestion of its modulations, this is how being appears indeed: entering under an unstable rule, that of the real, flowing through the ravines of the galaxies and the hidden stones of celestial bodies, just as it does over our own star, with shores without havens, on earth as in heaven, and flowing often upwards ("it would be to be"), starting after a while to flow downwards ("it was to be"), the cycle repeating incessantly.

Thus, turned within itself but knocking constantly toward fulfillment or sending things toward such fulfillment, this is how being appears to us, from the meaning of "to be *întru,*" within which there are limits but also absence of limits, advancement but also pulling backwards.

Limiting then the notion of being to the unilateral vision from the *Miorița* is a graceful but guilty renunciation. Compared to the gravity of being from other ontological conceptions, the fact that the idea about such a diverse and supple being could give someone the sentiment of detachment and thus make the Romanian human being to have a characteristic and mioritical lack of fear before death is only, let's say, beautiful rhetoric. The

5 The *Menaion* is a liturgical book in the Orthodox Church, which contains readings designated for each day in a calendar year. The *Menaion* is used in most daily services.

6 See I. Bianu and Nerva Hodos, *Bibliografia românească veche* [*Old Romanian Bibliography*], Vol. II (Bucharest, 1910), 236.

7 Noica's parenthetical note.

lightness of being is only the expression of freedom, almost exuberance that it receives in the Romanian view. The magic of being in our language says thus more than the gravity of gloomy, overwhelming being of some traditional ontologies. Such magic is, naturally, different than the predominantly artistic one of the *Miorița*.

Compared to the complex and magical being from our view, the neopositivist perspective of the Western world, which forgets being or sometimes reconsiders it in other philosophies, has an air of poverty.

When, on a foggy winter day you see the pale globe of the sun, you tell yourself, after all, it could be absent. This is what happens in modern analytic logic with being; its distant echo is maintained as a singular point only, namely the "individual constant." The logician could perfectly be without it, in his organized game with signs that don't want to signify anything on the level of reality and even on that of thinking.

The logic's diffuse totality from other contemporary views stands in contrast with the punctuality of being in logic. The sentiment of being would be this time—as in a new Pantheism or Spinozism—that of a total presence without any determination. However, an indeterminate presence becomes indistinct and is just as well total absence, as it has been said. Not only do we "forget" of being—we are told as a reprimand—but being itself retracts completely before knowledge, so that we can determine what being is not rather than what it is.

The Western logician as the Western metaphysician want surety: the former wants the surety of exactitude; the latter, a surety of absolute certainty.

The Romanian sentiment of being is different than the sentiment of ultimate surety—not regarding man's self-knowledge but regarding its apparition and state. The experience of being registered in our language would be, as we said, rather of the order of essence than of immediate and sure existence. This is why we preferred to say here pre-being at times for being, which includes both essence and existence; at the same time, though, we don't invoke the simple essence, because this gets separated from existence, while pre-being presupposes it and refers to it all the time.

Under pre-being we included:

— unfulfilled being, expressed in our language by "it was not to be";
— suspended being, by "it was about to be";
— eventual being, with "it may well be to be";
— possible being, with "it would be to be";
— the being of the entrance in being, with "it is to be";
— accomplished, consumed, fulfilled being, with "it was to be."

A reference to existence appears in all these modalities, as a moment of fulfillment. But the moment remains an end of a path, and the modalities are its steps of insurance.

For why must being appear in the hypostasis of surety and full reality (which can mean, for some, the simple "individual reality")? On the contrary, it is precisely *being*—in case it is not the sketchy one of individual reality nor the massive one of the presupposed absolute reality—that is the source of nuancing reality. Reality has more or less being, and respectively being has, in the bosom of reality, grades of fulfillment.

Faced with such nuances, the common exigence of obtaining being according to the model of sensible certitude ("I want to touch you and to shout out, 'It is!'" says the exasperated verse of a Romanian poet[8]) has something rough in it. On the other hand, there is still something too categorical and lacking nuances in the representation of an absolute reality that would confiscate being for itself and would say like Jehovah, "I am who I am," or in man's acknowledgement before God, "you are," in the sense of "only you are," which, historians say, is how the enigmatic letter E that had been founded on the frontispiece of the temple in Delphi should be understood. Being cannot be rendered by a "you are," by an "I am," or by some sensible ecstasy.

8 Noica refers to Tudor Arghezi (1880–1967).

These examples are at most exceptional beings. Being, though, is not an exception: it is that which is most common.

In order to have access to "that which is most common," which is being, Heidegger focused his investigation over a privileged existent creature, man. Man's speech is the protector of being, as the philosopher will later say, but even more, man as such, with his deeper approaches and his way of being in the world, could favor the revealing of being, we are told.

If being is conceived as permanence as that invoked by the ancient Eleatics ("there was what it was and there always will be"[9]) and as ultimate foundation to which all things and processes are reduced, then it is not man but rather the rest of reality that would reveal being. The inorganic, for example, shows clearly today that material being is, in final instance, an electromagnetic field. In the spirit of the pre-Socratics, someone may say then that its ultimate principle is something like a wave, just as Louis de Broglie[10] said once that everything was born out of the condensation of light. (Isn't saying that "everything is light" just as grandiose as saying that "everything is water," as Thales said?) If, on the contrary, you wouldn't think of the material being that constitutes the world, which is only element and is in change, but rather of a permanence like an absolute, then man reveals precisely the contrary to permanence, properly speaking.

Man does not reveal only being, but also everything that surrounds it. He himself pre-exists, for he is not only *in,* but he is also *întru* something. Man makes attempts, and he sees his

9 Noica refers to Parmenides's poem, most likely to fragment B8. The goddess tells the young man about the path that is: "a single account still remains of the route that it is; and on this route there are very many signs, that what is is ungenerable and imperishable, a whole of a single kind, and unshaking and complete." We are using here Patricia Curd's translation. Patricia Curd, *The Legacy of Parmenides: Eleatic Monism and Later Presocratic Thought* (Las Vegas: Parmenides Publishing, 1998), 68. Being is ungenerable (there was what it was) and imperishable (there always will be).

10 Louis De Broglie (1892–1987), French physicist, who won the Nobel prize for physics in 1929.

own limits, just as the limits of everything that is in the world; he enlarges the real toward the eventual, remakes it as possible, sees it in the immanence of its fulfillment as real, and then contemplates it in its accomplished reality.

These are not only his situations, but also the situations of being. Being itself is that which is not in stable settlement and is not an absolute. When Hegel, who invokes being as an absolute at the beginning of his *Logic*,[11] realizes that being as such cannot be anything determined — tree, man, or even the entire universe — and it cannot even receive determinations of a general kind, such as quantity or quality, he concludes that such a being, which is nothing, is the same with nothingness itself.

But how rigidly logic, how little Hegelian is this thought, that being is *either* something determined, and then it is not being itself, *or* something without determination, and then it no longer is. The Romanian experience of being shows that something can be said about it even when it is thought without any determination; that being enters in situations, and only these situations are determined. Then, being must not decay into nonbeing, as in Hegel, to then pass in becoming and reveal and unfold itself. Being reveals itself and makes itself known through its situations.

The Romanian sentiment of being is of something close, accessible, and with meaning. It is not about an absolute, nor is it about something irrational and ineffable, which would become accessible only by a sensible or intellectual intuition. Being has a foundation[12] and can be understood in its making, beyond its ready-made.

Higher thinking, which intersects the vast processuality of the world — not only of "what is," but also of "how what-is is possible" — searches not for being, but the becoming *întru* being. Thus, it encounters creatures that come into being or come out of being, creatures of a moment that still have part of being. Everything that receives that consistency of being in the

11 Georg Friedrich Hegel, *Wissenschaft der Logik* [*Science of Logic*], 1812–16.
12 Same term, *întemeiere*, translated above also as "grounding."

world of man — and one cannot refuse to the human world a certain fulness of being, in some cases — is after all a creature of a moment. But such creatures do not put the grounds of being less into play, being that is characterized not by permanence in eternity but by the fullness of reality.

The Greeks themselves could not remain at absolute being, and they put into play a less rigid being, but truer. This is how Romanian being wants to be. Just like the being of the ancient Greeks, it does not oppose nothingness; rather, it opposes something that belongs to chaos. Nothingness can be full of poetry (the heavens are open, in "Mortua est,"[13] and nothingness descends upon the world), but it is a curse for philosophy. Romanian philosophical sensibility has not fallen under this curse.

Chaos and Nothingness in Eminescu

From a Romanian perspective, then, we shall say that being does not appear from nor does it oppose something that belongs to nothingness; it appears from chaos and is opposed to chaos. Beyond the permanent fond of existence — which could be the wave, the light, the electromagnetic field, or who knows what element such as hydrogen — being gives ground to some creatures of a moment, such as the "lost worlds" from Eminescu's verse:

> Since then and until today, colonies of lost worlds
> Come from gray valleys of chaos on unknown paths.[14]

Anytime nothingness is conceived at the beginning of things, it disconcerts thinking and proves to be a false problem (as it was seen, perhaps, in the case of Heidegger's problem, "why is there something rather than nothing?"). Nothingness makes sense

---

13 "Mortua est" is a poem written by Mihai Eminescu, originally published in 1871. Mihai Eminescu, *Poezii* [*Poems*] (Bucharest: Minerva, 1985), 25–27.

14 Mihai Eminescu, "Scrisoarea I" ["Letter I"], the first in a series of five letters, originally published in 1881. Eminescu, *Poezii*, 86–90.

only at the end of things. They enter in nonbeing, and end in it; nonbeing is only the cessation of being, not a reality that would keep it in balance. (At the most, it can be an experience of conscience for the so-called "metaphysical" natures.)

In fact, nonbeing is only non-being, a concept that is as arbitrary and elaborated as "non-man," so everything that is not man, man's complementarity; or as artificial as Anteros for the Ancients, imagined as a completion of Eros. (When they used the notion of nonbeing, the Greeks did not think of nothingness but of undetermined matter, that which has not taken on form.) In fact, non-being says less than non-man, for being does not have any complementarity that is not, so doesn't have any possible completion.

The notion of nonbeing has power of suggestion only poetically, and poetry alone, or who knows what risked theology, can do something with the idea of a nonbeing from the beginning of things and then as companion of being. This is what explains that, especially under the influence of Indian thinking, Eminescu could, at times, give to being a special poetical expression and greater philosophical titles than it deserves. However, he doesn't invoke nonbeing either, at the time when he must give, even poetically, a more organized philosophical construction, even on Indian model, as it takes place in "Letter I":

> At the beginning, when being was not, and *neither nonbeing...*[15]

At the beginning was chaos. Thinking does not need to explain how being is possible faced with nothingness: it explains how being is possible faced with chaos. In a sense, it must be able to say, "Give me chaos, and I will show you how a world is possible." But chaos can have two faces: it can be a chaos of undifferentiation, of homogeneity, of equality of states as in modern entropy, or a chaos of universal lethargy (etymologically, "forgetting activity"); and, on the contrary, it can be a chaos of ex-

15 All of the italics in this and the following verses belong to Noica.

treme differentiation, total heterogeneity, as in "everything was together" from the vision of the ancient, a chaos of inequality and activity that is untied and contrasting at the same time.

It is odd that Eminescu begins, following the source that he has as inspiration, with the latter, the chaos of contrasts, and ends with the former, the chaos of total undifferentiation. He writes,

> When nothing was hiding, though everything was hidden…
> When *embued* by itself *the one unembued* was resting,
> Was there a *gulf*? An *abyss*? A deep *spread* of water?

Immediately, though, he will say, invoking a chaos of perfect homogeneity:

> The shadow of the things unmade had not started to unfold,
> And in peace with itself eternal peace was reigning!...

Under the obsession of consistency in thinking, someone might imagine (and such an intervention had been suggested, even if not in the terms used here) that these verses were erroneously rendered or that, in any case, a slight correction would make them in harmony with the beginning. In another version, one may imagine that the verses would be better rendered this way:

> The shadow of the things unmade *did not cease* to unfold,
> And *unappeased* with itself eternal peace was reigning.

Such attempts do not manifest an artistic impiety only; in the present case, it is also a philosophical untruth, since chaos can indeed take the face of homogeneity and that of non-homogeneity with itself or among elements. After all, Eminescu questioned the chaos of contrasts, which he invoked at the beginning, and allowed the reigning "eternal peace" at the end. Still, it is good to emphasize that, next to the chaos of eternal peace, there is also a chaos of differentiation until the end, since this second chaos will in fact return constantly in the bosom of being once being is constituted, and this chaos will give the beginning of all specific worlds, just as the original chaos gives the original world the power to appear. If the appearance of being from cosmic chaos has something exemplary in it, giving the model for the appearance of the formations from every plan by its steps of unfolding — from other kinds of chaos, as those of thought, of the beautiful, or of the good — then a form of chaos can be found, and it cannot be other, in the midst of the world, than the form of secondary chaos.

But how does being appear[16] out of chaos? Only here we must separate from Eminescu. You could accept his inconsistency regarding the vision of chaos because inconsistency proved to be only apparent; you will not accept, though, the genesis brought into play by the poet because it simplifies the paths of being too much, or it sends them to the miraculous.

The philosophical construction that the poet attempts seems to lose its rational control when he writes,

> All of a sudden, the point moves… the first and only. Behold
> How out of chaos it makes a mother, and it becomes the Father…

There is something privileged and, after all, miraculous in this genesis: in a certain moment ("all of a sudden"), a certain point appears to be active, "the first and only," as the poet says. Why this point? The privilege that the poet claims for this point is suggestive poetically but ends by raising questions regarding its entire genesis. It is true, any genesis in small and any creation in the world of man — which means that any plus of being on any plan — seems to be produced at times according to this model: at a certain moment, a point, whether in things or in thought, begins to move, something unexpected happens, and a creation

16 In the sense of "coming to be; getting to the point of being." But this does not imply the idea of becoming, so we avoided "coming to be."

becomes possible. However, this is a renunciation of any explication and not the attempt to provide one.

A single point, a moment, a subject — they represent always something privileged. But two points entered in a relation, no! The *relation* represents the great conquest of modern thinking which no longer sees privileged substances in the real but rather functions, as it was said; before making a conquest of scientific thinking, the relation is a situation of reality, which prepositions bring to light, particularly a preposition such as the Romanian *întru*. Any two points can be in relation, though, in the bosom of chaos; a certain relation can be created anyplace and anytime. There is no longer unicity, but, as unity of relation or original unity, it becomes possible everywhere, without keeping for its content any form of privilege.

In this hour of genesis, things prove to be just as human genesis appeared to an odd contemporary thinker, Teilhard de Chardin.[17] As an evolutionist scientist, this thinker could not see humanity's genesis from a single original pair, Adam and Eve, as the Biblical tradition wants, tradition which is respected by theology. Teilhard believed that the doctrine of his church would be contradicted in this single point, in the idea that several pairs of people came to be at the beginning, at the same time or independently, instead of only one pair. By this saying, though, this man of science contradicted, in fact, the entire religious doctrine of which he pretended to still be connected because he also abolished the miracle by nullifying unicity.

If being appears from chaos and transforms chaos into a mum, then the father also stays under the sign of plurality from the beginning, just as the seed does in late biological genesis, a genesis that must take place according to the model of the entrance into being. The science of being cannot remain at a single generating being nor at a privileged creation. Its problem is precisely the individual, the creature, that always takes the image of

17 Pierre Teilhard de Chardin (1881–1955), French philosopher and paleontologist.

many individual incarnations.[18] For, if one can no longer risk the idea of a Great Individual, which seems to give an answer for a moment, only to then reclaim the miracle for the genesis of the other individual creatures, then it must conceive the individual as a unit that does not have the unicity of the Great Individual, or of the "first and only" point.

It is not a privileged individual point that enters in movement, but an individual situation, created by a relation that can appear anywhere in the original chaos. In the universal untying, something enters into folding: and if it is not given to it to be in one part, it may well be to be in others. Now, the implicit thinking of Romanian language comes into play. It knows that ontology begins with the individual creature; however, unlike other languages, it doesn't merely say this point is, or this individual *is*. It says, it may well be to be in one or another of the certain valleys of chaos. It would be to be; it could take being.

To Take or Not to Take Being[19]

"To be or not to be" is a grandiose phrase, philosophically vain. "Why is there something rather than nothing," the saying attributed to European metaphysics, proved to be vain as well, after all. But "to take or not to take being," as our language says, has sense completely, just as, "why does something take being instead of nothing" is an admirable sentence with which one could open a treaty in ontology.

The science of being does not reach its target if it does not give account of individual being — of *this* tree, *this* man, *this* his-

18 The Romanian word for incarnation, *întruchipare*, is formed by *întru* and *chip* ("face"), so it would rather mean "in-facing," or receiving a face.

19 This expression could also be rendered as "To come to be or not to come to be." We chose to use the more literal "to take being" in order to avoid the connection with the notion of existence that is implied there. In Greek philosophy, we often find the idea that things that come to be and pass away do not belong to the impassible reality of being and are unknowable.

torical creature. But it must do it for any individual being, and so from the perspective of general[20] being.

But some thinkers saw being only in the individual, others only in the general.

The general by itself can say nothing about being. Why doesn't mathematics have the problem of being? Because it does not have the individual. Mathematics established itself in the general from the beginning and recovers its form of reality ("mathematics doesn't know what it's talking about," Russell[21] said, defiantly) only by its application in sciences and technology. Mathematized sciences, as astronomy or physics, have fully an ontological completion through their domain of reality, respectively through the individual realities (in a restricted or large sense) to which they are applied; pure mathematics is foreign to being.

If, however, the general alone can say nothing about being, the individual alone and individual realities cannot lead to being either. Brute recording of that which is through the five senses cannot be called ontology (it would be an ontology at this level: "I want to touch you and yell, 'It is!'"[22]). Just like the general alone, the individual alone does not reveal being.

Only the interweaving between the general and the individual give being, or, better said, the individual situation caught in or placed in generality. In this sense, the spherical and limited individual being of the ancient, but at the same time general and

20 We chose to use "general" to translate the Romanian word *general,* in order to be consistent with the Alistair Ian Blyth's translation of Noica's *Becoming within Being.* Another possibility is to use the term "universal" here. Noica's ontology is based on a triadic model: the individual, the determinations, and the general. Blyth chooses to capitalize all of these three terms, just as he capitalizes the word "being." Noica does not. While we see the benefit of doing so — we can separate these notions from the more profane use of the terms — we also believe that capitalizing them may suggest the existence of some entities (Being, the Individual, the Universal) in the rather Platonic sense of Forms.

21 Bertrand Russell (1872–1970), British philosopher and mathematician.

22 Verse from "Psalm VI" of Romanian poet Tudor Arghezi, which Noica has already mentioned. Arghezi's cry is directed to God.

not leaving rest[23]; or the Spinozist being, as an all of Nature, the unique substance, compared to which the rest of things represent only affections and modes; or, finally, a Great Individual, again unique but general, as Brahma, and so many divinities of an ultimate order — all of them could respond to the request of coupling the individual with the general. But the unicity of the invoked individual leads to the disappearance of that vision into theology or into myth.

This is where the notion of being that Romanian saying suggested with the formulas of the verb "to be" can come into play. There is nothing grandiloquent in this notion. If being represents "everything that is more common," then exceptional being, with its unique individual, can fall. The thinking of past centuries seemed to be, and it often was so, too solemn, speaking only about the ultimate principles, faced with ultimate reality. However, it can receive a lesson from sciences that were able to revolutionize knowledge only when they took in consideration a simple stone falling or a frog leg that twitches under electricity.

In fact, thinking practices such wisdom, in its good times, starting with Antiquity; it was not only Aristotle, who often is too excessive in the way in which he registers the brute fact and left it without transfiguration, but Plato himself, who asked whether a hair or dirt also had an Idea and who, after all, knew how to begin all his dialogues from a concrete situation, from common people and events, and then go up toward essences. But thought too often forgot this tradition.

From the folkloric level, Romanian thinking has practiced, as it was natural, such a lack of solemnity. In its cosmogonic vision, for example, the world is born of a worm or a butterfly. But even for superior levels, this thinking suggests measure, with its meanings of presupposition and with its investigation into the possible, together with the investigation into the real. Being is not only "it is," but also it may well be to be or would be to be, in

---

23 See B8 from Parmenides's poem mentioned in n. 9 above: "on this route there are very many signs, that what is is ungenerable and imperishable, a whole of a single kind, and unshaking and complete."

spread out zones; in our Romanian thinking which is infused in language, the elements, processes, and creatures in their transformation, far from having at times an ensured entrance into being, barely wait to take being and run the risk to not truly take being at other times.

However, the measure is also of the real, not only of knowledge. Not everything succeeds in the bosom of the real. If thinking must account for how the real is or was possible, then it must face the spectacle of the real's unfulfillments. There is a reject of being too. The treaties which unfold the making of things in a too-certain way, starting from above, from principles, or even from below, that is, from the elements, speak without having a genuine piety for their object. The part of disorder from the real must be understood and integrated in the presentation of the order of the real. For being, that which is revealing is not the appeal to the nonbeing that the moderns invoke too often; on the contrary, the unfulfillment of being is revealing.

Unfulfillment, the disorder that is, nevertheless, oriented, and those which do not reach the point of taking being, all of these represent, after all, states and processes that are more spread out than order and being. But these states and processes do not deny being. Throughout the known universe, there are crazy waves of all kinds that are running without getting to wrap themselves around a nucleus and thus give vast systems or infinitesimal atoms. Similarly, not everything from the vital plasma takes on being; the attempts to form a new species must have been immensely more numerous than the successful species. (Scientists, however, described only what is, not what tried, in all ways, to get embodied—what sent its polyps to one side or another to check the chances of taking being.) At more elevated levels, unfulfilled being is the ocean where, here and there, islands of successful being appear. In man's life and in his spiritual being, all sorts of attempts soar unceasingly, at times toward unfulfillment.

Just like in the Brownian motion of the particles in the vase with water, being prepares its apparition—after individual situations detach from the original chaos—in the framework of a second chaos. Beyond the generality of the original inertia or beyond the assault of all against all in the view of Anaxagoras, the aspiration to being — if not even the matter's and also the spirit's hazard that forms being — attempts to create individual situations which will be fulfilled or not under a new generality, which is now specific.

In this tension between an individual and a general, one can read the origin of that which "is to be." All sciences that man brought into play and his entire culture are established after all on the consideration of this tension in one or another reality field, so on the tension between the real and the law. Without the coupling of the individual with the general, culture would stay under the sign of entropy. Precisely this coupling is brought to light in itself by a universal science, that is, the science of being.

Nothing is foreign to the tension between the individual and the general, except the universe of pure mathematics where relaxation regarding being reigns. Transforming this universe and its methods into the exclusive key of knowledge means precisely refusing knowledge, as well as repudiating any meaning for being. Perhaps "to be or not to be" has meaning from a mathematical perspective, and it would even fall under calculation. In its well organized, probabilistic game, mathematical symbolism could just as well catch the opposition between something and nothing, and even the measure in which something can exist instead of nothing. But faced with a question with speculative ingenuity, such as, "does this individual situation take or not being?" mathematics must be quiet, while the rest of culture has almost everything to say.

The Rehabilitation of the Individual

In the Romanian sentiment of being, its creatures of an instant[24] are also included. The world is made of such creatures. Every-

24 The creatures of an instant, or momentary creatures, are the entities that survive only for a moment. Noica uses the term metaphorically as well: a

thing that has been embodied[25] is individual, submitting itself to becoming and disintegration. You may call the earth the Great Individual, as Hegel wants, or you can give this name to any galaxy. In its turn, life, where it takes place, represents the individual itself, while societies, facts, and thoughts have individual titles unceasingly.

The problem of being is relevant for such creatures of an instant and not for material or intelligible permanencies, which, if they were, can only be eternal. In this sense, modern mathematics has the probity to not ask the problem of being because any of its structures would have "being," just as it doesn't ask the question of the law, because any of its statements would be a law, and it doesn't ask the problem of truth either unless in specific limits.

Being, law, and truth have sense only for those things of the world of the "corruptible," as the Ancients used to say. Mathematics is incorruptible. However, contrary to those modern thinkers who forget the corruptible even after they started from it and dream to reduce everything to the mathematical incorruptible, the Ancients found the corruptible even in their "incorruptible," represented first by celestial bodies; at times, they may have felt the impurity of this astral order (the sun is a stone, an ancient thinker said[26]), just as their deities were tainted by the human. In any case, the Ancients were genuinely discon-

---

human being is a creature of an instant in the great scheme of things. As we can see further in the text, he calls Charmides such a creature.

25 We mentioned above that the Romanian word for "to embody" is *a întruchipa,* which is formed by *întru* and *chip* ("face"). The difference is meaningful: while "to embody" suggests a form that takes on matter, a întruchipa suggests that something, undefined, takes on face. This leads to a completely different understanding of entities; we may no longer speak of hylomorphic beings, constituted by the working together of form and matter but rather by entities (beyond the form–matter dichotomy) which take on being. The term *a întruchipa* also gives more strength to Noica's claims that everything is for the individual. An individual is something that has a face, in a large sense, that can be distinguished from others due to this face.

26 Possibly a reference to Anaxagoras, who claimed that the sun is a mass of fiery metal.

tent anytime they thought that, in the center of the incorruptible world, they were forced to place precisely the corruptible earth. On the other hand, the same Greeks, of whom people have reproached their tendency toward the incorruptible, brought the incorruptible into play in order to support the corruptible, not to dismiss it. In its good understanding, the Platonic Idea came to establish and strengthen the individual; substantial forms and Aristotelian matter were united precisely in order to make the individual possible, and the microcosm of the Stoics sustained, after all, human microcosm.

This tendency of the Ancient abstract and universal to descend to the concrete and to support the individual takes on delightful forms in Plato, where it seems as if you are promised only the elevation to the Idea, but at times you are given, through the Idea, precisely the wealth of the concrete. When he searches for the idea of youthful wisdom in the young Charmides, who gives the name to the dialogue, you don't really know if he obtains any Idea through that young man who is beautiful in body and thought or if the Ideas themselves come to describe Charmides as concrete existence.

This Charmides is a creature of an instance, but he has the right to being as well. Even more, only in such individual creatures can being be implanted in order to be something else other than a word or a thought. By itself, it's true, the individual is not; but without it, being would remain a word or an empty thought. This is why the individual must be rehabilitated, and the Ancients, who had the instinct of being, clearly prove that they also had the instinct of the individual. They, with their plastic sense, understood that being must enclose a measure and a tension.

We must then start from the individual in order to be able to say about being something other than it is in eternity. The individual itself has a past. It has detached itself from chaos, or it has denied, with its form of closure and determination, the chaos as disintegration. At the beginning, it can be a simple, individual situation: in the chaos of nature, it can be the vertigo made by two points that are caught in a rotation or the dependence of the variation of one of it on the variation of the other; in the moral chaos, it can be the bringing together of some behaviors meaningful for life; in the aesthetic chaos, it can be the accentuation of some images that are connected and some configurations that take on flesh in the indetermination of the world or of the imagination; in the logical chaos, it can be an implication and a reaction in chain. In any case, the individual represents a detachment for the universal release.

The individual is now suspended; it has detached from something, giving itself a proper face.[27] It came out of the condition and of the security of being in something. Here, though, Romanian thought can interfere in the ontological discourse, differentiating between "being in" and "being *întru*." The individual is suspended and watched[28] by nonbeing, but its detachment is oriented: it must enter in a form of "being *întru*," even with the price of actually falling in nonbeing. This is what differentiates the individual from the particular: a particular thing is in a given generality that it particularizes, while an individual thing is *întru* a generality and has a certain becoming in its bosom.

Everything that has taken an individual contour finds itself in this precarity. There's something positive here but also something negative. Eminescu, regardless of how intensely he may resent the negative, cannot avoid making space for the positive. He writes,

> Ephemeral flies of a world so small that is measured with
> your elbow,
> In this boundlessness we're spinning, forgetting completely
> How this entire world is just a suspended moment…

Of course, individual realities are suspended. However, the chances of being are, together with them. This is why Eminescu writes immediately,

27 A "face" is the translation of *chip*, the noun used in the verb *a întruchipa*, that we mentioned above. The individual doesn't take on a body ("embodiment"), but it gives itself a face (*întruchipare*).

28 In the sense of ambushed, hunted.

Thus, in the endlessly deep night of eternity
We have the moment, the radius, *which continues to hold…*

In order to make its appearance, being needs nothing more than such a defeat of a moment of the devastating time. Its sentiment is in fact the presentiment that, among those that fall, there also are some things that hold. As Udriște Năsturel[29] used to say, translating, "Whoever has not tasted the sweetness of those that are cannot understand the nature of those that are not." You must know to separate between what is destined to be and what is not destined to be in order to be a historian among the acts of the world.

About the Fields of Being

When a historian unfolds what was, he renders only a part of what was. Not everything that took place in the past has historical character; even if he knew everything, a historian would not keep and render everything.

Let us imagine now a historian who would have to decide in the present — whenever that present would actually be — what has and what doesn't have historical being. How can he leave aside one act, regardless of how insignificant it may seem? On the other hand, how can he accept all of them since some of them may be just dust and ashes? This is what happens in the science of being, which has before it the entire presence of the world.

Its difficulty does not consist in saying what is but rather what is *not* from among the realities that are. The problem of a thinker is the problem of a historian situated in the present: making a separation, stating that *what is* is, even when it is a creature of a moment, or stating that what seems to be is *not,* but has only the ambitions of being.

29 Udriște Năsturel (~1596–1659), Wallachian scholar and statesman.

Only in this context, when nonbeing is not a simple zero of being, meditation about nonbeing has sense. The question that was claimed to be central for any thought, "why is there something instead of nothing," invokes a zero of being. A less vain question would be *why is there something that is not nothing?* For it is possible for something that is a nothing to exist, something that, in a full, existent world, does not have the strength of being.

Reflection about being begins with such realities that enter in being so that they risk falling into nonbeing at any time. We identify them as individual situations, individual realities, simple points detached from the universal undifferentiation or caught in the universal solution. Being so, they carry with themselves chances of being. Their strength, and their first ontological investment, is to be emancipated from the original undifferentiation, one that can still be unceasingly renewed. We determine the individual as that which came out from the condition of being *in*.

Of course, this is a negative determination, stating, in a way, that the individual can be called that which no longer totally subsumes itself to the general. But the strength of the negative that Hegel mentioned can reappear here. Just as the individual is, as a simple point when compared to the massiveness of the general and as the undifferentiation or the chaos out of which it got detached, the individual has precisely the strength of being *întru* something. We can now recover Eminescu's verse:

> That point in movement, much weaker than the foam grain
> Is the boundless master over the boundaries of the world.

All the rest of the world has boundaries; if, exteriorly, there are no boundaries other than poetically ("the boundaries of the world"), there are inner boundaries for each element that departed from and was so widowed by the infinity of the general. That point of individualization is, however, "master over the boundaries of the world," in the sense that it carries within itself the unceasing promise of being. But the poet's verse says it too categorically: it *is* the master, while, in fact, it is only able to be so, it would be to be so.

This is the image that is suggested not only by our saying but also by science. For evolutionism, for example, regardless of whether it is confessed or not, there is an unstopped possible plus of being which begins from a minimal difference. Small differentiations, small detachments in the warm seas of the beginning—and in any seas, of any beginning—give vital plasma, in the bosom of which other small structures will lead to more organized configurations that will allow the apparition of new differentiations (such as chromosomes or codes) and that in turn would lead to real embodiments. This is how it takes place everywhere, underneath the life of organisms or above it. Isn't this about being?

That point of "movement," the poet says, however, is only one term in the economy of being. By itself, in its precarity of a foam grain, it couldn't give the measure of being. Still, thinking had to presuppose it as a small individual matrix in which being could inscribe itself. Now, starting from the individual, the idea of being is susceptible to receive rigor, even if not the symbolic rigor dreamed by sciences. There is a sort of rigor even in our formula, that the individual, with its promise of being, represents the commitment to a way of being *întru*. But this formula remains a simple suggestion for the moment.

At this moment, being can take its model from a different place than the suggestions of speech, and this is from the realm of scientific thinking. What happens to the individual? It gives itself free determinations, just as any individual that came out of the condition of an object and came into that of human subject gives itself some new, varied, and free determinations. A second term of being appears thus naturally, after the individual: the term of "determinations." The determinations of an individual, with their variety that is connected, at the beginning by only the constant presence of that individual, create a field. Before being in a static embodiment, being or its promise appears as a field in which determinations are the force lines of the individual.

It was said that the idea of field is the most significant conquest of the new scientific thinking. If, at the beginning, it was defined by physicists as a "region of the space in which each point is characterized by quantities that are functions of the coordinates of space and time," the field in science has today a rigor that the field of being cannot revindicate — at first. On the other hand, if we understand the field simply as an "environment created by points," as the physicists do, or the atom as a "point with an atmosphere of force grouped around it," the field of being can have kinship with them. Actually, a question is whether the idea of field must be the same in each case. There have been discussions of field of conscience, linguistic field, notional field, where there cannot be an analogy with the electromagnetic field. Each field, together with that of being, could have its establishment and its structure.

In this moment of its establishment when it is only the free content of determinations that an individual gives to itself, what is different in the field of being compared to other fields is the fact that it has an *open spatiality.* All the other fields have a certain and, to some extent, closed spread, even if they don't have an outline as well. By the determinations that the individual receives, the spread of the field of being does not have a stable spatiality at all, and there is no system of equations that could fix its structure.

Scientific thinking can project its formulas over all forms and even deformations from the material world, just as any random curve from a plan proved to have an equation; only one system of forms and deformations, the one of flame, could not yet be captured formally. The moment in which it is reduced to the individual and to its determinations, the field of being has something of this moving spatiality of the flame, as an embodiment that would grow and diminish freely. Will it catch on being, or will it not?

Beyond the individual and its determinations, there is one more thing needed so that being appears. The fields, as "swarms of light" the poet says, are attracted by something:

And in swarms of light that stem from the infinite,
They are attracted in life by a boundless longing.[30]

We cannot speak of *dor* experienced by inanimate matter, and we cannot speak of appetite, tendency, or formative impulse; but we can speak of an openness *întru,* which is also a closeness of individual determinations *întru* something, and we can speak of this for inanimate matter as well as life and spirit. The range of determinations of an individual stay or not together. The individual — the colony, the swarm of lights that affirmed its freedom — finds its necessity and is. Or it doesn't find it, and it is then listed among the "colonies of the lost world" of which the poet wrote.

Is it prescribed to some of the things to be, and to others to be not? Can the cipher of being be read from its enciphering, as still Eminescu says?

We have passed from a question and from the modulations of being to that which can be the Romanian sentiment of being, with its arborescence and orchestration, confronting it at all times with the visions from the great world of culture. The simple weaving, as natural as it seems to us, of implicit meanings in language and poetry, with the great explicit meanings of culture, can show us that the Romanian sentiment of being opens toward its rational understanding. There is a texture of being, perhaps a model or even an archetype, which our implicit thinking approximates at all times.

Being appears to us as complex, not only exteriorly by its arborescence and ramifications in different ontological zones, but also by its inner structure, which is perhaps the same in all modalities. In it, there is something heterogenous, not simple homogeneity: being is not without the individual, which, on its turn, cannot lack determinations, but each one of these are not truly without something of the general order.

30 "Longing" translates the word *dor*. See n. 2 above for discussion. In the following paragraph, we leave the word in Romanian.

What precisely is this cipher of being, which seems to be approximated by our sentiment at all times, is no longer said by language, and Eminescu mentions it only in passing. However, if we try to see for a moment the reason of being beyond the Romanian soul, we will return then to it, to its words, fairytales, and cultural creations in order to give a body to a scheme and life to the *archē,* which is being.

IV

The Reason of Being

A Model

According to the Romanian sentiment of being, then, it is possible for some things or situations to be, to attempt to be, to not succeed in being, to anchor themselves in the success of those that are, to be possible, to be in potentiality, to be about to be, or to be so well fulfilled in themselves that they would already be consumed and would already have been. In all of these, "to be" must have a meaning, and only one.

Let us attempt a rational reading in this good apparent disorder. It is indeed a disorder from the usual point of view. It can no longer be said — with an expression that would be in fact tautological if it were exact — that being means only "that which is." Here, the meaning of being must be of such nature that it would allow its elements to exist, even if being were not; thus, being would have elements, constitutive terms, and so structure. These elements have actually appeared in the analysis of the sentiment of being: they were the *individual* that was coupled with a general and gave itself or received *determinations*.

The fact that three terms can be at play is shown — even before their structuring into a firm model — by a famous saying of Antiquity, from its negative perspective. The Greek sophist and rhetorician Gorgias used to say that 1) nothing exists; 2) if it existed, it wouldn't be known; 3) if there was knowledge, it could not be transmitted to others. But what else is expressed in Gorgias's saying, if not, first of all, that there would not exist anything of a general order, and so that being would have to have a character of generality? Or second, that being couldn't be known even if it existed because it doesn't have an individual face,[1] and so it must have a form of individuality? Or finally, that knowledge of such being cannot be transmitted, which means that its determinations cannot be indicated, and so that it must necessarily have determinations?

If, however, these are the terms of being, then let us place them in order, as much as possible, starting from that individual without which there is no face of being[2] for the Romanian philosophical sensibility, and not only for it.

Something individual gives a determination to itself or receives a determination; determinations comprise a field around the individual. What makes this field *to hold* and what makes a new reality *to be*? Two or more points enter into a whirlwind; what makes the whirlwind become a star or a cosmos? A human gives himself various determinations throughout the day. What makes that day to have meaning for his spiritual life? There is need everywhere of a conversion of the determinations toward something, or *întru* something.

For such a conversion that gives foundations of being, it seems that examples can be found at any stage of reality. An atom is not achieved without the engagement of the electrons on the orbit which has a general sense; a chemical substance and an organic cell are achieved by subsuming the determinations of inorganic or organic matter to the generality of structures and laws. On the other hand, the subsumption may not take place: there are the so-called proteinoids, which have the entire substance of proteins, but they were not able to truly constitute

1 Recall that the word for "embodiment" in Romanian is *întruchipare,* and so it uses the word for "face," *chip.*

2 "There is no face of being" uses the same word *chip,* which can also be used in the expression, *nu e chip să…* that means "it is impossible to…."

themselves into proteins. There are organic substances that have all the letters of a code, but they could not institute the corresponding genetic code. First, as Darwin said, there are varieties, and only then from some of them, real species are accomplished with their genetic sense well insured. There are — and there were probably even more of them in the past — oral communications that could not give themselves a grammar, and thus they were not capable to enter in the generality of a language. There are, finally, historical facts and processes that have not obtained a general meaning and have thus not reached the level of historical being.

At any stage of reality, it could be shown that the entrance into being — of course, at that stage, we can deal with being at an inferior stage — is done by the conversion of the determinations of something individual toward a general.

We can encounter the suggestion of such a conversion on a page from Marx's *Capital.* It is the double scheme from the beginning of his work, regarding the passage from the developed form of the world of commodities to the form of the "general value." At the beginning, a commodity expresses its value through others. Thus, in the example from his work,

$$\text{20 yards of linen} \begin{cases} = \text{1 coat} \\ = \text{10 lb tea} \\ = \text{40 lb coffee} \\ = \text{1 quarter of corn} \\ = \text{2 ounces of gold} \\ = \tfrac{1}{2} \text{ ton of iron, etc.} \end{cases}$$

The initial commodity could be regarded as an individual reality that takes on different determinations; for, even if it is still about commodities, they come to determine, in a varied way, the value of the first commodity.

What happens in the economic process? There is a rollover that means, properly speaking, a conversion of all the commodities into one, respectively of their values toward a commodity considered as the general value. Now, we have

1 coat	=	
10 lb tea	=	
40 lb coffee	=	20 yards of linen
1 quarter of corn	=	
2 ounces of gold	=	
1/2 ton of iron	=	

The figure has been merely overturned, but something essential took place: a *general value* came into play. The fact that a commodity is equivalent with and is expressed through the others is not the same with the fact that all the others are expressed through and equivalent with it. The initial commodity fulfills a different function now. It has lost its individual character and has become a general value. Actually, it will give up the place to gold or to money, as effective general value. But from now the conversion came to change everything and to give economic being to the initial determinations under the sign of the general value.

We can now return to the ontological model. We recovered the individual and the determinations in this example and one other notion, that is, the general value. There are three ontological terms: the individual, the determinations, and the general. When the determinations of the individual are caught in a general, a new reality catches being as well. The conversion toward the general is that which gives being to the individual and to its free determinations. Let us choose the most expressive example: a man.[3]

When *is* man[4] (as man, and not at his lower levels, in his simple vegetability or animality)? Anyone of us has encountered or discovered a good definition of man. You may say, man is the only being that engages in sport, that is, he plays free of in-

3 We chose to use the word "man," and not "human being" due to the complications that the term "being" would produce in this context. "Man" should be read as "human being."

4 The question is odd, since Noica doesn't ask *what* man is, rather *when*. This is in the sense of, *when* does man obtain? When are the conditions for man to be?

stinct and age; you may also say that he is the only being with a tragic conscience or the only one that can cover the entire earth, as Teilhard de Chardin[5] thought, or the only being that gives definitions of this kind: man is the only being… Any of these characterizations of man represents a determination that, curiously at the beginning, can replace a definition. Isn't it curious for there to be hundreds and hundreds of definitions, each of them valid, after all, for a certain reality?

But there is nothing curious anymore, if you consider the nature of man as man and you see all of his possible determinations engaged in this nature. Such a *ratio essendi* has been well known and named for a long time: man is a "rational animal." Nothing else could be said about the being of man as man. Even the character of irrationality can be definitory for him, and I have intentionally chosen the sentiment of the tragic, just as we could have chosen the absurd, in order to say that even the irrational relates to man's rationality. Dialectic knew how to clearly say this, by its permanently exceeded contradictions, showing that even that which seems "irrational" from the simple perspective of the intellect is no longer thus from the deeper perspective of reason.

All those free determinations, which can be unceasingly many, were converted in human rationality, which envelops them and can bring other determinations, giving the status of being to man. The figure was thus, with any other determinations:

Man {
- Plays freely
- Has tragic conscience
- Is able to spread throughout the earth
- Defines and defines oneself
- …

5 Pierre Teilhard de Chardin (1881–1955), French Jesuit priest, theologian, and philosopher.

The figure can also be overturned, and the determinations can be caught in something of the general order, which would give them the necessity:

Playing freely Having a tragic conscience Being able to spread throughout the earth Defining and defining oneself …	characterize *man* as rational being

The conversion toward the general is that which gives being to the individual and to its free determinations. What happens if the conversion to the general doesn't take place? Then there is a reject of being, as in the case of the proteinoids which never reach the stage of protein, of the varieties that do not become a species, or of the sayings that do not become a language. In that case, being is not obtained, at least being at a certain level of reality, as the human level was in the invoked figure. The individual can give itself and can receive any determinations (as the empty whirlwind of material points, or the empty spread of waves), but it doesn't truly have the measure of being.

The world can be filled with this secondary nonbeing; this secondary nonbeing is not striking in the world of inanimate matter, because it is precisely the secondary being that is the rule here, while being is the exception; in the world of life and of man, though — which cost matter so much effort to coagulate — nonbeing and unfulfillment are in a sense a true cosmic failure. This only means that the conversion has not taken place.

It seems, then, that the ontological model resulting from here is simple: an individual (I) opens through determinations (d_1, d_2… d_n…) which open under a general (G); an ontological field receives being and insurance, by becoming a field of the general. Schematically, it would look this way:

$$I \left\{ \begin{array}{l} d_1 \\ d_2 \\ \cdot \\ \cdot \\ \cdot \\ d_n \end{array} \right. \qquad , \textit{but} \qquad \left. \begin{array}{l} d_1 \\ d_2 \\ \cdot \\ \cdot \\ \cdot \\ d_n \end{array} \right\} G$$

However, the figure says too little about the genesis of being. First, the model is static, as if the individual would be already unfolded according to its determinations, and their conversion *întru* something general would also be given. But if the model cannot be static, it is not dynamic either because it must express only an overthrow. We could say that the model must be "anastrophic" (from the Greek *anastrophein,* "to overthrow"), running the risk for the individual to end up, catastrophically, by its collapse into nonbeing, just as the proteinoids and the varieties. But how can you create a figure of such implantation of the individual in the general, implantation that seems to be the only one that can tell us what being *is*? For, on its turn, being once reached is accomplished being, and in fact, it "accomplishes" itself properly speaking, and it fades out slowly. The being of matter also has a disintegration, the being of biological species has an evolution, while the being of man, as incarnation of him, leads to historical creatures only.

Second, the model sins by the determinations inscribed in it. On the one hand, the individual gives itself determinations that do not have an ontological significance at times (as, for example, spinning around purposelessly or the non-integrable acts of man's day); on the other hand, if the individual carries within it the uncertain infinity of possible determinations, the general opposes to them its infinity; the good one, the infinity of determinations that, at this time, hold and get structured together. No configuration can show that in one case it is about bad infinity—with the exception of Hegel—so the infinity of "more and more something," while on the other side the infinity of the controlled possible is at play, the infinity of both this *and* that.

Third, the model sins when it presents the general as something given, as the Aristotelian substantial forms and the Platonic ideas appear to be given or, on a different level as the awaited Godot is given in the play of our contemporary Beckett, and Godot is a prototype perfectly homologous with a general nature. But precisely in one of the best accentuated versions in that of biological species, the general is not already given — unless in a large sense and for the needs of scientific categorization — but it is realized at the same time with that which is made by it, which means that the species evolves as well. The general can give being even if it *is* not. A general nature such as language, with its spirit, barely has a shadow out of the consistency of the species; the general of a work of art, the thought which you want to embody, no longer has anything beyond the accomplished work that absorbs it.

We must now return to the suggestions of the Romanian sentiment of being. If there is a dram of geniality in the bouquet of meanings of our preposition *întru,* it is because it precisely expresses the situation in which being emerges by the opening toward something that may also not be.

"Being *întru*" may mean an opening toward something given, but it can also mean the opening and the self-organization under something that *is* only by this opening and this organization. Thus, things can be "*întru* a fulfillment"; but they are not on the way toward it (for fulfillment "is" not) but rather on the road *with* it. When being receives embodiment, only then the generals appear. When the individual specimens reach a definite contour, the species emerge. It is as if earth gives itself its own heavens, as some mythologies say.

In this sense, for speakers of Romanian, we could say that understanding being and attempting an ontology that can give account of the real world — a world that has creatures of an instant, but it is also imbued with the fullness of being at times — means to bring to light all that is implicit in the preposition *întru*.

There are some implicit contradictions in being that give it a special tension, on the one hand, and a good sway, on the other, between interiority and exteriority, rest and movement,[6] as well as having a hold and having a lack of something. To swing and a swing—Sextil Puscariu showed in his *Cercetări și studii*[7]—come from the basket that was "swinging" from the ceiling.[8] Perhaps the most moving and fecund contradiction from *întru* is the one already mentioned, which is to express the oscillation toward something still unknown. Being, with its swinging that we have seen in Romanian modulations, emerges by anchoring into something that often doesn't even have a name.

This is how we found it in its model; this is how, after all, a few great spirits of the past have conceived it; or this is how we encounter it—as a fulfillment of the life of the spirit—in some great sayings of humanity, among which we place one from our Creangă.[9] Among his sayings, he notes a strange one, perhaps taken from people, or perhaps his own, which sounds this way: "It must have already come, since it no longer came." On first sight, it is a joke or one of these expressions that belong to resignation. But what if it is something else than this? For it is sufficient to bring the notion that it *either* comes *or* it doesn't, from Beckett's *Waiting for Godot* and, in fact, from the mentality of the West, to see that it is not resigned wisdom only that is at play in Creangă's saying. That which you wait to come—which can be your happiness as a human or the good solution for you and

---

6 We used "rest" and "movement" to translate the Romanian terms, *stare* and *nestare*. *Stare* also designates a state, while *nestare* the nonbeing in a state.

7 Noica's parenthetical note in the Romanian edition: Sextil Puscariu, *Cercetări și studii* [*Research and Studies*] (Bucharest: Editura Minerva, 1974), 34.

8 Noica makes the connection between the Romanian words *leagăn* ("swing") and *a se legăna* ("to swing"), on the one hand, and *a lega* ("to tie"), on the other. The swing was tied and hung from the ceiling, so Noica says that the word *leagăn* comes from *a lega*.

9 Ion Creangă (1837–89) is a writer who is most famous for his *Amintiri din copilărie* [*Memories from Childhood*] (Bucharest: Cartea Românească, 1941). He was a good friend of Mihai Eminescu.

your world, or whatever else it may be — cannot always have the character of a determined thing which may emerge or not; however, by the simple expectation and openness toward it, as I have shown, it represents something that may have even come to model the face of your being and of things, as an unseen hand; or perhaps it is there as a beneficial presence, as Creangă said, even if it remained unknown.

Words such as these travel through the model from above. It seems it has already come, since the awaited order has not come. This order commands to us a way of searching, precisely because we have found it. In its fertile ground, it takes over all of these words and meanings and makes them give fruit to the word *întru*. This word belongs to Creangă's language and does not represent the expression of rest or resignation since it says that everything that is sends further *întru* that which is, just as everything that you have found out is an occasion for further research. This is why we will be able to say that the deeper model of being, just as that of the life of spirit, which is connected with being, is not reduced to a scheme, be it even anastrophic. The deeper model is a preposition — *întru*.

"The Evening Star" and the Model of Being.

Two creations, Eminescu's "The Evening Star" and a folktale, "Ageless Youth," could illustrate the ontological model drawn above, stemming from the Romanian sentiment of being. As we will see, these two creations exhibit more than an illustration of the model; they also deepen and accentuate it. In "The Evening Star," one can glimpse its meanings through unfulfillment; in the folktale, through fulfillment.

Truly speaking, Eminescu began his work from a folktale as well. It may be that, unlike any other form of artistic creation, a folktale has an ontological meaning in itself. It represents an artistically organized attempt to describe being, which is invoked at various levels of reality and non-reality. The narrative, the drama, or the lyric do not usually search for access to being because they are too involved in a human's adventures and disasters. A fairy tale operates with humans and stereotypical situations, and so it speaks of what is and could be, about what it was and what it was not to be, about what among things possibly is, something that "wouldn't be told if it were not."

Even if it springs from a fairy tale, Eminescu's poem has not been understood ontologically, in being but rather much too often psychologically, in that which is human. The discussion has descended so much into what pertains to the human aspect that we arrived at Brătescu Voinești's[10] interpretation, which was allegedly accredited by Maiorescu[11] and which represents an offense to the spirit and, after all, a disgrace for artistic receptivity. The writer mentioned above said that the poem would be about Eminescu's love for Veronica Micle, "who had fallen in the chains of Caragiale-Cătălin" and about the "paternal intervention of the demiurge Maiorescu." When Perpessicius[12] mentions this interpretation in his edition,[13] he shows that the facts invoked as support are not even exact.[14]

Then, if "The Evening Star" was allegorically about the genius, according to Eminescu's own suggestion, Eminescu couldn't

10 Ion Alexandru Brătescu Voinești (1868–1946), Romanian writer and politician.

11 Titu Maiorescu (1840–1917) was one of the most influential nineteenth century literary critics. He was a founder of the *Junimea* Society, where Mihai Eminescu first read part of his work.

12 Perpessicius (1891–1971), Romanian literary critic, who edited Mihai Eminescu's works in a multi-volume edition to which Noica subsequently refers.

13 In a parenthetical note, Noica mentions Volume II, p. 37.

14 Noica refers to one of the most famous love stories in the history of Romanian literature. Eminescu met Veronica Micle, his greatest love, in 1872 in Vienna when he was about 22 years old. She was also 22, but she had been married for eight years and already had two children. Her husband was thirty years her senior. The alleged story mentioned by Noica refers to another love triangle. Ion-Luca Caragiale, a famous Romanian playwright, is said to have had a love affair with Veronica. Titu Maiorescu, the most important Romanian literary critic of the period and a protector of Eminescu, has allegedly intervened.

talk about himself. For him, in "Scrisoarea I"[15] and all of his manuscripts where he writes about the genius, the genius was first of all a learned man; he knew very well — and the manuscripts show it — how much he still needed before he could consider himself a learned man. For him, the genius was also someone in whom anyone could "hide his own features"; however, he could not believe that he expressed the thoughts of people in general, other than by a successful verse, as he could not consider himself a true pioneer, being under the humiliations of his tumultuous life.

Was the poem about one possible sublimated experience? Perpessicius said admirably, in the same work: "Of course, any lyrical creation [...] is connected with a life moment." But he adds, "However, this does not mean that 'The Evening Star' does not have a great and unsettling problem beyond its immediate data."

For this great and troubling problem (we don't enter in the literature about the poem, which is huge and contains so many Romanian and foreign remarkable interpretations), one could invoke in the past the romantic view of the world beyond the psychological aspect, that is, the aspiration toward an untouchable ideal. But what a platitude! And how uncomfortable you feel if you remain at the level of this interpretation, when you accept that the supreme success of Romanian poetry — for this is what "The Evening Star" is — rests on such a background of romantic platitude. What remains, then, are those admirable isolated poetic moments, while the whole leaves you that bittersweet taste of the banality that is superiorly poetized, as it sometimes happens with Goethe's *Faust*. Perhaps this is why, you tell yourself, "The Evening Star" has not succeeded to conquer in any of the translations in other languages, where the enchantment of the Romanian verse is lost, and what remains is the poetical basis, which is so precarious. And you may perhaps add

15 Mihai Eminescu, "Scrisoarea I" ["Letter I"], the first in a series of five letters. originally published in 1881. Mihai Eminescu, *Poezii* [*Poems*] (Bucharest: Minerva, 1985), 86–90.

that this is the fate of romanticism and of any form of exaltation of the spirit, to fall at times in great banality; it happened to Novalis[16] as well, to Hölderlin,[17] and to Eminescu himself at times, in some page of literary prose.

Let us leave aside the good taste, which doesn't know to say more than this, and let us see if, in its thematic content, "The Evening Star" says more than it first appears to the philistine in each of us. Eminescu's simple notation on the story that he was versifying could lead to false interpretations, if it was badly read: "The allegorical meaning I gave to it," he wrote obliquely on page 56 of the manuscript 2775[B], "is that if the genius doesn't know even death and his name is freed of the night of forgetfulness, then here, on earth, he is not able to make someone happy, nor to be made happy. He doesn't have death, but he doesn't have luck either. It seemed to me that the fate of the Evening Star in the story is very similar to the fate of the genius on earth, and I gave this meaning to the allegory."

Two things are to be retained here. First, it is not directly about a genius, but about the fate of the Evening Star (it remains to be seen what sense of existence must be given to it), and the fate of a genius is "very similar" to it. We must emphasize this "very similar," which means less than "it resembles," just as "I love you much" means less than "I love you." Second — and this is the deciding thought that should eliminate from the beginning the romantic platitude of the aspiration to an untouchable ideal — in the poet's interpretation, there is no trace of the impotence and the misery of the earthly soul to raise to an ideal but rather, and movingly so, of the misery of that general and superior nature, which is the genius or, in the story, the *Evening Star*.

Indeed, this is where we must start, from Hyperion. What is Hyperion? It is "hyper-ion," the one that walks on the above, in Greek, the one who is not fixed in an individual situation, like all of us but who passes over our destinies — just as the great mean-

16 Novalis (1772–1801), German romantic poet and philosopher.
17 Friedrich Hölderlin (1770–1843), German poet and philosopher.

ings of man's history pass — with his general nature. Thus, it is a general nature, a spirit, a "soul," as any star for the Greeks, but a soul that now doesn't even have the stable generality of the other stars, but it wanders like a planet or a wandering star, in its pure detachment from everything. The fairytale says that, for a moment, the desire to be caught into something is given to it; the entire poem describes the unhappiness of the general because it is not able to take being truly.

There are, however, generals that take being, so they take an individual face, just as there are individuals that are caught into something general, and then they lead to being as well. Indeed, this could be the fairytale of being or its model: an individual gives itself determinations that are caught into a general nature; or a general is determined, specified, and embodied.[18] Let us give names, then, to the interpretation in being that "The Evening Star" can suggest, following what we mentioned above: a general nature, on the one hand, gives itself all the determinations that are possible for it. An individual nature, on the other hand, meets it with its own determinations, with its call and its self-sacrifice; but their determinations do not meet, and the model of being is not accomplished. Or, in the terms of the Romanian modulations of being: an *It may well be to be,* in its swinging from the world of the general, and an *It would be to be,* in its swinging in the world of the individual, stretch out their hands toward each other, but their hands do not touch.

What is striking in the poem is that, from the beginning, the individual creature proves to be serene, and she will remain this way the entire time. She is a simple and most beautiful girl, not even an emperor's daughter but coming from high kingly families, and as she rests in her human innocence to watch from the window in the evening the apparition of the *Evening Star,* or as she sees or rather feels his night, his light, "Descending on her

18 In this case, Noica no longer uses *întruchipa* but *întrupa,* the proper translation of "to embody."

closed, large eyes, / And covering her face,"[19] she is overtaken by *dor*.[20] However, both in wakefulness and in dream, she is serene, while he is not.

She looked at him with a slight smile,
He trembled in the mirror…

Turmoil doesn't belong to her but to the creature of light. As she is buried in the darkness and the sleep of her individual nature, the maiden feels clearly that she cannot come out of her condition; however, she wants to transfigure it. The individual creature can request from the general just as much as the girl requests, that is, to have her life illumined. It is as if, from the beginning, the poem passes responsibility for the good encounter on the general. What can poor individual creatures do other than to open themselves toward it, *întru* it? It is the lot of the general natures, just as that of general meanings (the genius is the only one that knows about them) to bend, by people's call, in such a way as they transfigure their lives. What the poet describes from here on are the vicissitudes through which the general goes to become reality.

First, the Evening Star is embodied out of the Sky and the Sea, "A dead man with lit eyes from space." He came with difficulty from his sphere, he confesses, to follow the earthly call and to ask the girl to be his bride. But she sees him as an angel only. How could she walk on angelic paths? Still, she continues to call

19 The complete translation of *The Evening Star* can be found at the end of this volume, in the translation of Octavian Gabor. Eminescu's poem has been translated before. See, for example, Adrian George Sahlean's translation, *The Legend of the Evening Star,* in his volume of translated poems: Mihai Eminescu, *The Legend of the Evening Star: Selected Poems* (Global Arts Inc, 2021). See also Leon Levitchi's translation in Mihai Eminescu, *Poezii* [*Poems*], bilingual edn. (Bucharest: Teora, 2009).

20 See chapter 3, n. 2 about the Romanian word *dor,* meaning "longing." As mentioned above, someone has *dor* for something that she has known and no longer has. In this context, the *dor* of the individual creature for the general creature sounds as if the individual has had an acquaintance with the general prior to the moment when the general takes on determinations, so the general is something even if it hasn't been embodied.

him in her earthly sleep, for it is given to an individual creature to look for its law, its meaning, its bridegroom. This is why the poet himself says, "She *had* to bring him back to mind, / The Lord of waves unshaken."

The Evening Star thus struggles to find a new embodiment — thus, the general nature, meaning, law searches for another entry into the real — and comes "in sadness, and pensive," with difficulty, once again, to tell the human creature that he was embodied from Sun and Night, this time, with the thought of taking her with him. Fascinated once again but holding her own, she no longer sees him as an angel but as a demon (perhaps because he has part of night in him). She had called him, it's true, but she doesn't understand his call-answer: "Although your sounds I do record, / I cannot comprehend you." It is not given to the individual creature to understand any call of the general but only that which can assume it as it is, in its individuality.

Now, the worlds are separated, to the rawest contrast, to the incredible opposition between human whimsicalness and cosmic gravity. Eminescu had the courage to oppose these two paintings[21] poetically. Remained alone without the assistance of the law, the individual falls immediately, almost into triviality. Cătălin appears as well, an out-of-wedlock boy from the streets, a common creature of clay just as the child from Goethe's *Prometheus,* who hit with his whip in thistles and who didn't know about love (about fulfillment, transfiguration) more than the vulgarity of adolescence taught him. Even the girl falls into vulgarity, saying as any girlie, "go about your business... leave me alone." But precisely when she falls into the carelessness of common life — "She rejects him, she accepts" — something comes to elevate her being once again: the thought about the Evening Star. At Cătălin's encouragement ("And if my face to you bends

21 One other possible word here is "images." Noica uses the term "paintings" figuratively, and this can be done in Romanian, where an image of the world is a painting of that reality. It suggests agency from both the world, which provides its being, and the one who, by observing this reality, creates a "painting" of it.

down, / Respond to me with your face"), she answers with the longing that the Evening Star awakened in her.

He penetrates with his cold rays
From a world that I now flee…
Forever I will sing his praise
Forever far will he be…

All of a sudden, evoking him, the painting of the world is changed, and a completely different scenario emerges. In contrast with the banally and even trivially idyllic world of some children, the wing beat of the girl brings a world of essences. But how alive, how original, "as in the first day," are essences under the plum of the poet! You can liken the journey of the Evening Star toward the Demiurge-Father only to Faust's journey to the Mothers, in act I, part II; and if the likeness must be done poetically as well, we will say without shyness that the desert invoked by Goethe as Faust's aim truly pales next to that of Eminescu's hero:

There is nothing; still, there is
A thirst that now absorbs him,
A depth akin to an abyss;
Oblivion. No more beam.

What can the Evening Star request from the great Father? While Faust requested the image of Helen from the Mothers, so an *essence,* Eminescu's hero wants *existence,* with its chaos, with its rest ("And from the rest I'm, born, no doubt, / I'm thirsty of some hiatus"), thus with the rest *întru* existence. Here, in his precipitation, he betrays the fairytale of being or its model, just as Faust, with his precipitation, betrayed the ideal of patient submission to the object of knowledge that belongs to any genuine learned scholar. This is because being doesn't mean the burying and the death of the general in the world of passing things but their fulfillment *întru* and by the general, even if these things are passing and the general remains, in its way, eternal. "The Evening Star" requests, though, just like Faust, to become something else than a creature of a general order (something else than a genius); the curse of the world — a world which is deprived of its great meanings when they, through their representants, the geniuses who cannot be bent according to the measure of the world scarcity — is that it remains a world of the blind becoming, which is the simple becoming *întru* becoming.

This is what the demiurge, the Father, tells the Evening Star. He knows better than the star through what balance between the general and the individual true being is possible. He tells him that the world in which he wants to sink is a blind becoming *întru* becoming: "But even if all people die, / Again, more people are born." "When waves in life find their tomb / More waves again appear." "And if a sun loses its ray, / And dies, it's back tomorrow." "For if one's born, one also dies, / And then returns from hollows." Isn't this clear to Hyperion?

Of course, if he didn't ask to be another, but rather to be himself *in a different way,* then yes, being would emerge in the world from the good encounter between the general and the individual; or this world from below, without which there wouldn't be, though, life would take truly being. His Father tells him, "And you, Hyperion, remain / Regardless of your sunset." He is a general nature, and he can only remain this way, even if he goes to sunset.

However, he can be a general nature in many ways, as still his Father tells him. He can be as wisdom ("Should I give you wisdom?"), and then the marriage with the world of the earth is possible; he can be general nature as the spring of art and its magic, just as Orpheus ("You want me voice to give this mouth?"); remaining what he is, he can be a law that masters and well organizes the world ("You want, perhaps, action to show, / Much strength and also justice?"); finally, he can be an earthly All-Conqueror ("I'll give you fleet, mast next to mast"), of course, in order to quench and not to stir the warlike craziness of the world. General nature can be so many things, in the chaos of the world, precisely in order to take the world out of chaos. In this manner, one may get from the becoming *întru* becoming to the becoming *întru* being.

What an extraordinary lesson does the father give to the Evening Star! He doesn't tell him, "we are doomed to remain cold and immortal."[22] On the contrary, he gives him numberless keys to come out of the lethargy, that is, forgetfulness of action, of eternity. But the Evening Star here is a Cătălin of the Heavens, or perhaps an exasperated Faust, who would be content with only a moment of happiness. Just like the angels from another Romanian legend who no longer wanted to leave the Earth, he would be ready to transform himself into a simple firefly, only to have "an hour of love." And because the Father knows him, he encourages him to gaze below, on earth.

On first sight, one would say that what takes place down below would justify the Evening Star's revolt. On the contrary, what takes place there under earthly guilt, is something delightful: the two of them stay together "under the crowns of lindens' lace," and the easy-going, worthless, and good-for-nothing Cătălin, the seducing adolescent, is overtaken by poetry as if transfigured by the light coming from the soul of the girl, which reflects the light of the Evening Star:

The sweet delight of your cold light
My thoughts gently refashions,
Eternal silence you do write
On my night filled by passion.

This is what the scatterbrained, the Dianatic (from Diana, as Haşdeu has suggested) said. How come does the Evening Star not see the work that he has already begun on earth, beautifying the life of the two?

What is even more seducing — and what the exasperated Evening Star–Faust doesn't understand — is that the girl, around whose shoulder her lover barely placed an arm "She'mbraced

22 This is not a quote from the poem, but rather a reference to what Hyperion says in the last stanza of the poem.

him with her graces," this earthly girl, drunk with the night, youth, and love, all of a sudden upon seeing the Evening Star, finds herself again in her human nobleness, and she exclaims, in the arms of her lover: "Descend, oh, gentle evening star..."

Thus, her earthly love no longer has meaning for her; the individual creature wants the other love. Now, she no longer tells the Evening Star, "transform my life in cheer!" as two times before, when she had called him, but she tells him, "transform my luck in cheer!" As any individual creature, she remains under the sign of luck, of chance, of contingency. Only general nature could bring necessity. But under which necessity should a creature from below find its order? Which should she invoke? To which law should she become a bride?

To this openness, so pure even in its staining, the Evening Star responds with his blindness of himself, which had not been dissipated even by the great Father, in his lesson. He exclaims, "What do thou care, oh, face of clay / If it's me or some other?" But this is precisely what the girl had asked of him, to enlighten her luck, her contingency, and to tell her if *he* is truly the expected bridegroom or another; to tell her what her necessary sense of love is. For you cannot think, when the Evening Star declares, "me or some other," that he wants to say, "me or Cătălin." Regardless of how much you would consider him a Cătălin of the Heavens, it is absurd to believe that he could place himself in balance with an uncalled from below, whom the girl even lost, due to his paucity, under the long line of lindens. "Me or some other" can only be a general nature or another, a general sense or another, a law or another.

The world of necessity and the world of contingency have not encountered each other. But they have *searched for each other.* If the Evening Star goes back into his unhappiness of being "cold and immortal," the world below has truly learned to raise its eyes toward him or toward another like him, as if it would be on the verge of breaking this small circle in which only luck takes place.

Only now the explanation given by the poet about the allegorical meaning of the poem gains its clarity. The fate of the Evening Star is the fate of the genius, Eminescu says; he cannot make anyone happy, and he cannot be happy. But for him, the genius does not represent a simple hypertrophy of the ego, as the nineteenth century wanted at times, in its common psychologist view; rather it represents that ego that has found out that "there is something deeper in us than ourselves," thus the ego that has found its own self. The genius is that who knows about the general meanings of the self, about laws and necessity. If the genius resembles the Evening Star, it is because it carries within itself the general, at whose level it wants to raise the world of luck. It cannot descend into this world, even if it desired it for a moment. To raise completely the individual to order, to law, to general (to make Cătălina a star) is not given to it. The unhappiness of the genius is thus of an ontological order as well. For the genius knows of being, while a common man does not. The world should take being, through the genius, but it remains a world of contingency.

However, the passing of the genius though the world, just as Hyperion's passing — the walker-above[23] — leaves behind a trace of light and a rumor of order. Eminescu's passing through our world brought such an extraordinary order and instituted so much being, despite the unhappiness and the disorder that belonged to him! Today, if Romanian being holds, even if the measure is not fully clarified yet, it is certainly because Eminescu passed through this world.

Thus, something special takes place in the world below, a world that the genius could not save in the way he wanted. Even more, something unbelievable takes place: this world from below comes itself to save the genius, just as Faust was saved not by his faith or scientific and worldly achievement, but by the mercy of Gretchen.

At the end of Eminescu's poem, you remain with an unclear sentiment of harmony, despite the disharmony between the two orders, that of the general and of the individual. Why harmony? Because while the order of the general has been frowning and agitated, the order and the disorder of the individual and of the

23 One possible translation: the Skywalker.

earthly remained with serenity — in the ontological terms already mentioned, we would say: with the goodness of "being *întru*" — under the sign of openness, of self-giving, and of transfiguration.

Of course, as simple as he is, Cătălin is serene because he doesn't know. But the girl *knows,* and she is still serene. The Evening Star is unhappy, but he didn't make her unhappy, as Eminescu believes the genius would do. Without wanting it, perhaps, he has created in the girl on earth a splendid exemplary of femininity, superior or naïve but also detached. She doesn't stay under the judgment and pre-judgment of the society, as Gretchen, who asks Faust if he believes in God, having in mind the God of marriages.

She is a Gretchen without Gretchen's writhe, a nature free of any constraints, all of a sudden above eros, which she doesn't know but doesn't refuse either. If she had a child, like Gretchen, she would not have thrown him into the well. She errs but aspires further. And she continues to wait, as all things that are individual, for the bridegroom, be it immortal but not cold.

We have, so far, a first illustration of the ontological model in Eminescu's "Evening Star." What I think we gained due to this illustration — even if it couldn't make a place for itself among the valid interpretations of this Eminescian poem — is the lesson that we received from the poet for our ontological method and its enrichment through an aspect that we could not guess from the beginning: the vicissitudes of the superior term from our model, the general.

The vicissitudes of individual realities, too earthly as they often are, surface from the beginning. If at first the model of being was affirmed, starting from an individual that gives itself determinations which were susceptible to be captured or not into a general, then it was natural — both in principle, as in the examples from nature or history — for the determinations of the individual to end up untouched by a general and to not be gathered together by its order, remaining a pure spread and, after all, a self-disintegration of the individual, if not a truly failure of being as mentioned.

Now, though, with "The Evening Star," a surprising ontological situation emerged, with or without the explicit will of the poet, who, after all, was merely remaking artistically a fairytale of our people. This ontological situation has the nature to show how much life and diversity are in the structure of the model, and what surprising inner symmetry it possesses in the moving balance of the individual with the general through determinations, and how justified we were for not relying on the usual rigid scheme but searching, just as Romanian language encouraged us, for that which is in the things *themselves*, respectively that which is in the self of such a model.

"The Evening Star" came then to show the vicissitudes of the general in the model outlined on the basis of the Romanian sentiment of being. You could believe that the general is a simple human idea, or if we put it more largely but more vaguely, a simple ideal that is accomplished or not. However, just as we found examples for the vicissitudes of the individual in the objective reality of nature, with the proteinoids that didn't become proteins, with the varieties that cannot become species, so they cannot rise up to the level of the general or with the sayings that do not become languages, we similarly find now, upside down, generals that are perfectly foreign to human ideation, that pre-are in things and do not succeed to catch on being by embodying in an individual situation.

Indeed, we can clearly see that, in the bosom of nature as detached from man, there subsist, there must subsist in a way (but how?) laws that have not found their application and may never find it, just as the Evening Star could not find its appropriate embodiment[24] and had to remain cold and immortal.

---

24 Noica has used throughout the chapter on "The Evening Star" the word *a întrupa* for "to embody." This is the first time he uses *a întruchipa,* which we discussed above. The two Romanian words can be used interchangeably, and Noica may use here the latter in order to avoid repetition. However, it is meaningful that the Evening Star, when it descends at the call of

With surprise or even with amazement, if we reflect deeper we find that new realities appear in the world during critical times, realities that are perfectly structured and defined, so they cannot be simple improvisations of nature. It is sufficient to have a few rainy days, properly speaking, and lots of insects appear, which previously were nonexistent in the biosphere; naturally, you ask yourself, if under a slightly changed atmospheric or geological regime (which is possible at any time), a completely different biosphere may appear. It is just the same in the order of culture or of spirit.

Coming back to Eminescu's poem, you tell yourself that, without wanting it, the poet gave expression to this very situation in which an entire world of generals is situated, ready to irrupt in reality, not being lazy, as the possibles that Leibniz's divinity doesn't use after it made its world the best of all possible. "The Evening Star" from the poem is merely one general case that is about to catch being, a case that is found in the demiurge's provision of generals. Without realizing it, you tell yourself that Eminescu may have given expression to a situation that is striking when it is noticed, even if Eminescu didn't realize it himself.

Still, did Eminescu do this without being aware of it? Let us assume that it is so in the case of "The Evening Star," which he took from a fairytale. But the fairytale itself is Romanian, and Eminescu's choice was not by chance. In fact, why would we search for indirect reasons for connection? There is a direct reason: the theme of the generals of the Evening Star type, which succeed or do not succeed at other times to penetrate in the real and thus to institute full being according to the model is a perfectly Eminescian theme. It will indeed be the theme of the arche,[25] which Eminescu himself will bring into light.

It will be sufficient to weave the idea of the hero from "The Evening Star" with the idea of the *archē* to show how Eminescian is the problem of the vicissitudes of the general, how appropriate

---

the young Cătălina, takes on human face and takes on individuality, but only in passing.

25 See chapter 5.

is the choice of the fairytale, and, finally, how Romanian is everything: the fairytale, the Eminescian poem, the *archē,* and — if we can take things to their end — the ontological model that we outlined.

We return to this model now after we saw it disconcerted, at the beginning, by the struggle of the individual that could not obtain its being by a good "encounter" with the general; then, in "The Evening Star," by the struggle of the general that couldn't "obtain" being by a good "encounter" with the individual either. Now, we find the model in its balance and equilibrium, but not without a quiver here too, with the astonishing Romanian fairytale, "Ageless Youth and Deathless Life."[26]

The Fairytale of Being and "Ageless Youth"

You can only be amazed by this fairytale. It is such an accomplished balance between extremes, such a rigorous ontological affirmation — and, as it will be seen, an affirmation of genuine being, not of that being instituted in a vain zone of eternity — and, finally, such a happy expression, that, for a moment, you remain before it as if before an unhoped gift that our folkloric culture brings to humanity. Who fashioned it? Where does it have an equivalent? For it should have one, in the worldwide literature of fairytales.

In Lazăr Șăineanu's impressive and unmatched work, *Basmele române în comparațiune cu legendele antice clasice și în legătură cu basmele popoarelor învecinate și ale tuturor popoarelor romanice,*[27] the author writes about the type of fairytale of "Promised Fairies," "Thus, this is the first fairytale from Ispires-

26 See the translation of the fairytale in the appendix to this book.

27 Lazăr Șăineanu, *Basmele popoarelor învecinate și ale tuturor popoarelor romanic* [*Romanian Fairytales in Comparison with Classical Ancient Legends and in Connection with the Fairytales of the Neighboring People and of All Romance-speaking Peoples*] (Bucharest: 1895).

cu, 'Ageless Youth and Deathless Life,' which, under its *full form, seems to be unknown in European folkloric literature.*"[28]

The fact that it is the first fairytale that Ispirescu gathered and edited seems fully symbolic to us. Did he, though, register it as such? Did he, a typographer who became a scholar, give it this expression without doubt? Did centuries give it this expression?

In any case, I don't know another work in prose of the Romanian genius that has so much substance, from the first to the last word, and such rigorous writing or saying.[29] I wouldn't dare to interpret any other Romanian work in prose, verse by verse, as I plan on doing or as I am *forced* to do with this fairytale; this is the only one which does not have a positive ending, as it has been observed, and still the only one that expresses, not indirectly, as any other fairytale, but directly, the fullness, the measure, and the truth of that which can be called: being. It is truly a "liar the one who doesn't believe it," as the fairytale begins.

But how could you not believe, when it is about what is, what you are, and what becomes on this world? The emperor and the empress are both "young and beautiful," as all of us, after all, at one hour of our lives, and they desire, like all of us, once again, to enter a good becoming *întru* becoming: to continue and to prolong themselves, having children. There is a luminous face of becoming *întru* becoming, not only a blind and dark one, as the one the Demiurge described to the Evening Star. After all, if you don't know of becoming *întru* being, if you are not able to raise things and your life to that fulfillment of being that, humanly, would give you a kind of "eternally renewed puberty," as Goethe said about the genius and the creator, meaning that it would give you precisely ageless youth, then what remains for you is the common human lot, regardless of whether you are an emperor or a common subject, to become as man *întru* a further becoming, just as you learn a few things in order to make another one to learn, you live to make others live, and you acknowledge, still together with Goethe, a prophet of the becoming *întru* becom-

28 Noica's parenthetical note in the Romanian edition, p. 395, our emphasis.
29 "Saying" because it first belonged to oral literature.

ing and for whom this becoming takes the place of being, that the only meaning of life is life.

Usually, mother Life takes care to place life in the world, and so a species takes care to maintain itself, by that *stirb und werde* of the previously invoked prophet, so connected with the spirit of Romanian folklore, even in expression, as it shall be seen soon. If, however, Life doesn't achieve this feat by itself and nevertheless life appears, it means that something more special can be at play — and our story is born here, as in the stories of the Old Testament where some women could not have children and, when they succeeded to have them, in old age like Sarah, it was about an exemplary nature in what is human.

Thus, here as well, becoming *întru* becoming, with its innocence and clear linear unfolding through the chain of generations, is interrupted. It is like a rumor that something special might happen. This is why the emperor and the empress talk to more distinguished characters, going to "healers and philosophers, to search into the stars and to divine whether they will have children."

At first, it is a recourse to the absolute instance for the people of nature, to the cosmic instance (the gaze into the stars). However, in order to be fulfilled, being doesn't need absolute instances, and even the emperors of fairytales — respectively, the Romanian sentiment of being — appeal at last to instances that are closer and better bearing of reality than the stars and evening stars. This is why the emperor doesn't shy from going to an old man from "a nearby village," no more than that.

How clearly does the old man tell the emperor that "your wish will bring you sadness." But why this? Because the moment when becoming *întru* becoming doesn't unfold its chain by itself, so the moment when the child is brought onto the world beyond nature, he will belong to a different order than the one which could not conceive him and will thus bring exception in the law and, respectively, in the blind flowing of life. "He will be

Făt-Frumos[30] and loving, but you will not enjoy him," the old man says. Indeed, he will aspire to something else, to being, let's say, as all the children who weren't foreseen in the civil state of becoming *întru* becoming. He will take his flight just as Euphorion, the son of Faust and Helena.

"You will not have him," just as the absolute pair of Goethe did not have their son. It is delightful and unforeseeably true that, in the artificial way of the construction in Act 3 of Goethe's piece, the great shadows, Faust and Helena, become genuine humans once they are married, even most careful parents, imploring their child — Euphorion, in whom the author liked to see a simple Lord Byron — to not aspire too high and to not take flight into the air.

But Faust and Helena don't have their child because he collapses, while the emperor and the empress from the Romanian fairytale don't have Făt-Frumos because, on the contrary, he is fulfilled beyond their destinies. We have here something that shows the difference between the rigidity of a part of Western culture that belongs to either-or — either we go up to heavens with the Gothic towers, or we won't be saved; either Godot comes, or he doesn't — and our view, with the delicate nature; still, more durable than the stone and the categorical imperative: of being itself.

What takes place now, when the babe is about to appear against or beyond natural laws, is highly significant for what we have called the Romanian sentiment of being. *Întru* appears, unexpectedly and unhoped for, that *întru* which seemed, after all, to be the key or rather the hidden nucleus, the intimate self of the model of being. The babe doesn't want to be born. "Before being born however, the child started crying incessantly, and no wise man could make him stop. Seeing this, the emperor promised him all the goods in the world, but nothing could make him stop crying." *Întru* what could he be born?

30 *Făt-Frumos* is the appellative of many princelike characters from Romanian fairytales. "Prince Charming" is one possible translation.

This motive of the babe who doesn't want to appear in the world, without knowing *întru* what he comes, returns in some Romanian fairytales, but it seems that not only in them. In the chapter already cited, *The Types of Promised Fairies*, Şăineanu writes, "*I have not encountered in any of the foreign collection of fairytales* the initial motive—promising a fairy to the child so that he stops crying—although it returns to our stories often. It deserves then at increased attention, as we couldn't give parallel versions to other peoples for the variants of this group."[31]

It seems difficult to believe—and still, this is how it should be, if indeed the vocable *întru,* with its richness of meanings that are concentrated in it, is specific to Romanian. Appearing in the world, if it doesn't take place blindly and under the somnambulism of the simple becoming of things and life, must be *întru* something—just as a human's creation, when he undertakes it and thus increases the world in the bosom of the world, must be also into something. Otherwise, why would creation appear, which is always a fulfillment and an exception?

But the king in the story doesn't know, at the beginning, about exception, and he promises the rule to the babe. He promises him earthly rule: "Be quiet, my son, and I'll give you this and that land"; but the babe doesn't get quiet. "Be quiet, my dear, and I'll give you a beautiful princess to marry"; but the babe doesn't get quiet and refuses to be born because everything that he is offered is his mere integration in the simple order of the becoming *întru* becoming.

Thus, his parent throws some foolish and unthought words; he knows or at least feels that they can be tempting to the babe since they take him out of the usual order: "Quiet, my son, and I'll give you Ageless Youth and Deathless Life." Only at that moment, when he found out *întru* what he was to be born, the babe "turned silent and was born."

This expression, "turned silent and was born," is extraordinary. This is a true expression for all the exceptional comings

31 Şăineanu, *Basmele popoarelor învecinate şi ale tuturor popoarelor romanic,* 359. Noica's emphasis.

into the world, particularly for the creations within its bosom. Any creation is born out of a cry and out of a silence. Of course, everything that is life is born in labors; but, for common life, a cry and silence are also common, while here the babe's crying is uncommon (how could he cry and how could this crying be heard from the maternal bosom?), and silence belongs to a different gestation than that of nature. You feel the struggle and the cry in the thoughts or even in the life of a creator, and then you seem to hear his silence. Something cried in Bach before he composed a *Passion*; then he was silent, and the *Passion* was born.

Born, then, *întru* something special — in this case, *întru* the expectation of being itself under the image of ageless youth and deathless life — the young son of the emperor enters the conditions of the unusual from the beginning: "he learned in a month what other children learned in a year." However, the king remains in the condition of the usual, in that law of becoming *întru* becoming that Goethe defined with "*stirb und werde*." The story says that the king, seeing what a wonderful babe he has, "died and resurrected out of joy." This is all he can do, as a common man, together with the entire nature: to die and resurrect, but not to overcome himself as man.

This game on the meadow of Life was played, of course, by everyone around him, for "everyone in the kingdom was proud because they would have a wise and skillful king like King Solomon." But the poor noblemen forgot that the same Solomon the Wise was also the Ecclesiast, who lamented the spectacle of the vanity of things and that he could not take his wisdom further than the contemplation of the deserted becoming *întru* becoming of the world. He didn't have the rumor of being (unless, perhaps, under the image of an angry God), and he remained somehow "not-skillful" in his wisdom. Such a model wasn't fitting for the king's son, who, once he comes into age, becomes "pale and sad, deep in his thoughts," precisely because he has the rumor, even the promise of being, and not because he would see, like Solomon, the vanity of things and nothing beyond them.

This is why he says, "Father, the time has come to give me what you promised me at birth." It was only normal to happen what was to happen, that is, the king became very sad, as the story goes. It appears that he shouldn't have been saddened but rather to have been a little ashamed — if parents can be ashamed for a lie said to children — because he had deceived his child when he promised him "such a thing unheard of," just to attract him to life. But the father is truly saddened because, independently of the fact that he cannot keep his promise to his son, he knows or at least feels that the being he had invoked, which was really unheard of and unfindable anywhere in the world, is meant to take out his son from the common world of becoming, at least due to his longing for it, with the opening *întru* it.

We find here, unhoped for, once again, an already mentioned feature of "to be *întru*": the preposition *întru* may open toward something that is not. The simple opening, though, models the subject that is in act, even creates the general sense *întru* which the opening was made. This Romanian fairytale rediscovers thus all the incidents and implications of the ontological model, even this strange situation in the process of coagulating being, which the model presented imperfectly and which could be justified only by *întru* with its silent works.

Thus, since the son was born under the sign of "being *întru* something special," for he would not have entered life otherwise, he must search for something he doesn't know well what it is; but he must do it under the rule of this saying: "you would not have searched for me if you hadn't already found me." He tells his father: "I am *compelled*[32] to roam the entire world until I find the promise under which I was born."

How precisely does the story express things! For it is written here: "until I find *the promise,*" so not something well known but rather the thing promised at the same time with the promise. At this moment, the king's son could tell himself, together with Creangă: "It seems it has already come, since it hasn't come."

32 Noica's emphasis.

And he is about to start looking for that which he has already found, resettling himself from a level of reality into another.

The others, however, remain on their level of reality, which they cannot overcome: "All nobles and servants kneeled and begged him to stay..." And what do they tell him? This: "Your father is old by now, and we will place you on the throne..." They even tell him directly, "We will bring you the most beautiful queen under the sun as wife." *This* is the perspective they can oppose to being: marry him, so that he would also have a child and would further pass a kingdom to this child. The "unfulfilled" courtiers promise to him, the one thirsty of being, to have a further continuation, to fall completely into the becoming *întru* becoming, and thus to enter the endless rotation of the world.

The king's son does not want and, in fact, can no longer enter that which only spins, in circles, since he is "born" under the sign of being. He is in another order, in the one of the one-who-makes-meaning,[33] where lives and things are said more deeply and better. In the name of this meaning that the son pre-senses, he is unwavering in his decision, "remaining true to his word, inflexible like a stone." Perhaps there is something foreboding in this word, "stone"; you understand the son's steadfastness, but his stone-hardening you might not, if the encounter with the reality of the stone-hardening *întru* being and not of becoming *întru* it would not be about to come, some place where the king's son is about to arrive. But let's allow the story to flow further, as a river over its rocks.

Now, when nobody can stop him to search for his promise, Făt-Frumos must find his paths of access to it and his tools. "Făt-Frumos went to the royal stables that housed the best horses in the kingdom to choose a horse" and, of course, as in

---

33 This expression doesn't fully encapsulate Noica's term, *rostitor*. *Rostitor* contains two other words, *rost* ("sense") and *rosti* ("to say"). As it is seen in the continuation of the paragraph, Noica uses this term, *rostitor*, with both meanings: the-one-who-says and the-one-who-makes-meaning. It is, we suggest, Noica's Parmenidean stance: "there's one thing for being and saying."

any fairytale, the one he chooses will be a horse with glanders, which, in reality, carries inside enchantedness.

However, regardless of the stereotypical character of this detail, we can see a more adequate meaning to the story of being: to reach being, you must not choose kingly paths. Being is born modestly, as Haşdeu used to say about the golden words of a natural language that were created "in huts and hamlets." You need dedication, in the way in which the horse with glanders (in fact, his own conscience as a pilgrim of being) teaches him: "You must take care for me with your own hands for six weeks, and you must give me barley after you boil it in milk." The simple aspiration to being must give us measure. Indeed, it is still his good conscience that tells him to not choose new or shiny clothes and weapons (perhaps a divine shield, like Achilles'), but "the rusty weapons and clothes of his father's youth." For, after all, the young man searched for his being; but this is connected back to his parents, those who gave him earthly being.

With such rusty weapons — but they were *his* weapons, his line's, and his place's — weapons for which he needed six weeks to make them shine again, Făt-Frumos is ready to start his great journey. But does one undertake a journey on uncommon realms? No, because it is rather about an ascension, such as Euphorion's, into the air. If his wings were meant to break — because he didn't know toward what he was ascending, since he was, like his father, Faust, or perhaps like Lord Byron, a wanderer without aim — the wings of Făt-Frumos, or the wings of the horse since they form together a body and soul, are such that they make him fly truly to *some other place.*

The others, his people, try to keep him here, in the world of becoming. "With tears in their eyes, they begged him to give up this journey so that he wouldn't end up going toward the ruin of his life." They sense well that this departure could also mean death, but they don't understand well the kind of death that is at work here.

Only after he "was outside of the kingdom's borders and reached wilderness" — not another kingdom but wilderness — only now can separation be consummated. He gives up everything that could still tie him to the world of common rules: "Făt-Frumos sent the soldiers back, kept only as much food as he could carry and divided the rest among the soldiers." He started toward east, so toward the great origin, toward the world of the beginning and of the ever-beginning of the dawn.

Now the trials of the pilgrim begin. There are three trials to which he is submitted, and each of them, on its own level, says something about the exit from the natural world. They are as three curses of this world against the one who leaves it.

First, it is the curse of the immediate world from which he just detached himself. Symbolically, the cruel Gheonoaia,[34] on whose realm he arrives, is a being who "used to be a woman like all others," but she had fallen under her parents' curse, "because she disobeyed them," just as, after all, Făt-Frumos stopped listening to his parents. The fairytale has the discretion of not making his parents, in their sadness that they are no longer listened to, revolt and curse, but it places before the son a first trial of facing a creature that has been cursed by its parents. Făt-Frumos confronts her and is about to win, but at that moment Gheonoaia asks for mercy. In order to be believed when she promises that she wouldn't hurt him, "she writes with her blood," the story says. We are still within the world of the making of people out of blood, and thus blood represents the supreme assurance.

Proof for the fact that the world of Gheonoaia is an echo of the parental world is the fact that she "invited Făt-Frumos to choose one of her daughters as his wife. They were all beautiful like fairies." Thus, just like his parents, Gheonoaia calls him back toward something of the order of becoming. The fairytale shows then that man can fall again at any time in the order from which

34 *Gheonoaia* appears in other Romanian stories as well. The name originates from the term *ghion* (*Dicționarul Explicativ al Limbii Române* — DEX [Bucharest: Academia Romana, 2016]), which designates a bird, the woodpecker. The word seems to be connected also with the Greek adjective *gēinos*, "earthly." The young son of the king has just detached himself from the earthly world, and the first trial is the earthly one. Perhaps, though, Gheonoaia, through her trials, may peck some of the worms that still inhabit the earthly body of the prince.

he has detached himself; our lad, though, open *întru* fulfillment as he is, does not fall back.

The second trial, or the second curse, is the one of Scorpia,[35] Gheonoaia's sister. She is cursed to be separated and in terrible enmity with the being that has the same blood as her, her consanguine being. If Făt-Frumos had to face the indirectly expressed curse of the immediate world, now he faces the curse of the *far*-close world of the consanguines, from whom he had also detached himself when he came out of the condition of the becoming *întru* becoming.[36]

That we have here an echo of the worldly *relatives* is shown by the fact that, the moment when he is about to overcome her, Scorpia also gives surety with her blood, just as Gheonoaia before (and it is perhaps significant that Făt-Frumos had cut only a leg from the latter, which he put back afterward; in Scorpia's case, who has several heads, as people have several relatives, he severed one of them, which he also put back afterward); this relative is more distant (contrary to the parents, who desire to prolong their species through him), which can be shown by the fact that Scorpia would no longer bring him three beautiful girls to lure him to regain Life and marriage *întru* that which is worldly.

After the trial that stood under the sign of the parental meanings that Făt-Frumos trespassed and after a second trial under the sign of largely human and tribal meanings also trespassed — for all of us humans are consanguine, after all — the third trial comes; it could also be the third curse, the one of the world of beasts and nature itself. Făt-Frumos wants to betray all of them with his aspiration of transcending his condition.

All three trials are thus born from the fact that man comes out of everyone's condition, of those close to him as of those further away, even of those in the larger world of nature. All must rise against his decision, either by praying him to remain

35 In fairytales, Scorpia is a feminine monster, having several heads.

36 Noica's note in the Romanian edition: In the two detachments — from family and from man's peers — as in the third that follows, the detachment from ensouled nature, one could see the archaic character of this fairytale, born into a world that tied man by codes and well determined customs.

among them as they do at the beginning, or by cutting his path as Gheonoaia or Scorpia do, or even by menacing him with annihilation.

The wildest menace is that of wilderness itself. Just around the palace where ageless youth and deathless life dwells (the fairytale speaks in singular, as if it would be about only one single person), there are the armies of Nature, which Făt-Frumos had ignored in the name of Being. "The wildest beasts in the world stay there. Day and night, they're on guard."

What do they protect? So that no one comes out of the enclosure of nature. And, because "there is no way to fight them" since you can fight a Gheonoaie or a Scorpie, but you cannot fight all Nature, Făt-Frumos will have to wait for the moment when he could go above the jungle of nature. He is an Euphorion who knows above what he flies and toward whom.

What a marvelous thing is shown to him when he passes over the wildest beasts in the world and when he is about to descend! "Făt-Frumos barely touched the branch of a tree. Suddenly, the whole forest shook, and the animals started hollering in a most frightening way." The forests themselves move as they do in *Macbeth,* nature goes mad, the beasts howl, and everything rumbles because of the trespassing that is about to take place: a man is on the verge of breaking the circle of his human nature.

But all of a sudden, when they, man and horse, or the flyer with horse wings, "came down," the scenario is changed as if by magic. What happened? We passed from the world of nature to the world of being. The beasts of the forests, wilder than anything else in the world, are now cubs, to whom the Lady of the palace, the great Lady, gives food. From the perspective of being, this is how all the dragons and the evils of the world are: some poor cubs or some beasts that now the Mistress "tamed and sent away."

In the hands of Being, everything becomes good and wise again. But if the beasts can be better again, man, who can be the evilest beast of all, is also that which can be best among the great Lady's cubs; his apparition gives her joy, for she "had not seen a human soul there." The Mistress rejoices then, and she doesn't punish the one who comes to eat from the tree of Life.

How can you not be still? And how can you not remain still a human, in your stillness, just as Făt-Frumos, who now sees that "the Mistress was a tall fairy, thin, delightful, and most beautiful!" And that's it. She's not a dazzling divinity of beauty and light; there is no angry God that appears before man's son; it is neither the spheric Being of the ancient Parmenides, with no eyes, hands, and voice, because it is "perfect," and so it is *not,* regardless of how much the ancient would insist on claiming that we can only say about it that it *is*. A beautiful creature appears now, a creature as you may believe you would find around our earthly places.

Far from frightening the others, with the thunder of her voice, the lovely mistress looks at him "with pity,"[37] the tale says. Did she have pity on him because he came out of the condition of man, of ordinary man? Did she have pity on him because of what was expecting him? But this cannot be because he arrived where he wanted and where no one arrives, the tale says. That which awaits him is only the lot of all humans, in the worst case, prolonged over centuries and centuries, though, as it shall happen. It is not pity in the sense of compassion, but mercy as goodness. Being itself is gentle, in its tender nature, according to this Romanian fairytale, and its words are inviting[38] and not at all final truths and decrees.

The mistress and this king's son talk simply: "What are you doing here?" she asks. In its discretion, the tale barely shows something, like a small shyness of the young man (there is no shock before a *mysterium tremendum* or a *mysterium fascinans*).

---

37 The Romanian *milă* could be translated with both "mercy" and "pity." Noica plays on this and starts analyzing which of the two meanings is suggested here. As it turns out, it was pity in the sense of mercy.

38 Noica has just criticized Parmenides for proposing a cold Being. However, his words here should bring him closer to this ancient philosopher. The goddess who takes the youth by hand in his poem is similar to Noica's description of the mistress here. She invites the youth gently, showing him the path of persuasion "for it attends on truth."

For, instead of answering the Mistress by affirming his person, so first person singular, he seems to be a little shy since he answers, "We are searching for ageless youth..." And the mistress is gentle and doesn't create problems by asking, "Who is we?" The horse and he? He and the rest of humankind? She answers graciously: "If you[39] are looking for what you[40] said, it is here."

It is here! Such a strange and new word! The mistress doesn't say, "It is *me*," and so she doesn't say like the angry Lord of the Old Testament, "I am who I am." She says, it is here. But it is she who is the incarnation of the searched ageless youth. Even more, she is not only its incarnation, but also the dispenser of ageless youth. She is Being.

Still, it is not her — not *only* her; for in the Romanian view of the world, Being has isotopes. As the young man enters the palace (palace? It could have been a beautiful hut just as well), he "found two other women, each as young as the other"; each as the other, just as the isotopes of the world's substances are some as the others. Just like the isotopes, though, the women are not truly alike all three, for these two were the elder sisters compared to the first mistress, the tale says.

Better than considering the isotopes of being, with its three incarnations, let us think back to the modeling of being into a structure, into an ontological model, where we also had three terms, three forms of incarnation. The individual was first, then its determinations, and finally the general, also with its determinations, which made the model of being to lead to being when the determinations of the general were covered with those of the individual — as it was not the case in *The Evening Star,* but as it is the case, at times, in the large world.

All of these three ontological embodiments are sisters, or — if the individual and the general are not fraternal from the beginning — they fraternize by one's determinations that overlap the other's at the hour of the happy occasion, the *kairos* of being. Among sisters, there must be *one* younger: the individual. The

39 "You," plural.
40 "You," singular.

other two, the older sisters, can be "one as young as the other," which means that, in the happy case of the fulfillment of the model of being, you can no longer differentiate between the general and determinations, for the general pours unceasingly into determinations and they gather unceasingly in the order of the general. It was necessary, then, that only one of the sisters was younger, the individual embodiment, the only one who is active in the real, gives food to the cubs of the world, and can speak from the beginning with people, individual beings as they are. The king's son truly found the ontological model, the archetype of being.

Now, when the son of man became the Son of Being, and its girls rejoice in having human companionship — man having somewhat the right to be their equal, contrary to the beasts, who are only cubs in the garden and area of Being — the scenario of any Genesis is recapitulated: the animals of the world pass before the new Adam, so that he would give them names. Of course, the girls let the horse (his part of mediation, his carrier toward another world, a good daimon, who mediated and traveled between one world and another) "to eat wherever he liked." Indeed, the mediator has no need to appear, unless Făt-Frumos, who knows, will desire to go back at one time, becoming again a son of man from a son of being. The other animals, though, had to pass before him, and even if the tale doesn't say, like Genesis, that he gives them a name, it shows that his companions of ageless youth "introduced them (him and his horse, him and his tool!) to all beasts so that they could walk in the forest in peace." Everyone reconciled into being. All is good.

But not all was good *there* prior to the coming of Făt-Frumos. The women prayed him to dwell with them from then on because "they said *that it got ugly being all alone*."[41] What a strange word, true somehow. For, in fact, what was "there"? No one had

41 This expression doesn't fully capture the Romanian. The Romanian *li se urâse* suggests a certain boredom. We wanted to maintain the word "ugly" because of the way in which Noica analyzes the expression further in the paragraph. Nevertheless, a better expression would be, "they got tired of being all alone."

access to the world of being (thus, the girls were staying "all alone"), and boredom has passed through the kingdom of being, our Romanian "ugly"? "What is the ugly made of? Of the man who is silent," the Romanian says. There, everything was silent. There was no human, no speaking world, no acts, no determinations — or there were the same determinations always, in the terms of the ontological model.

These girls were not really the so-called *dii otiosi,* those lazy gods who retired in their heavens after they made the world and seem to no longer know what to do from then on. But the girls of being were not doing new feats either, or nothing was bringing them out of the boredom of ageless youth and deathless life, and so it got ugly.

But their ugliness of an eternity could not be yet, from the first moment, ugliness for Făt-Frumos as well. This is why "he didn't need to be told twice, and he received gratefully, since this is what he wanted anyway."[42] This is what people have searched for steadfastly, ageless youth, and they asked for it from nature, from the gods, from medicine, from astrology or biophysics, they asked to be given days without number. Let us see, though — for the fairytale didn't want to stop at this happy shore — what happens to those who, like Făt-Frumos, lose the count of days.

First, it was as good as possible, since novelty is pleasant even, or especially so, to those settled on eternal life. Thus, "slowly, they learned each other's ways," and this work of good habituation, of good match between new man and new man, is indeed a delight. But it ends soon. Then, Făt-Frumos "told them his story and what happened to him until he arrived there." What can beings who have nothing to do do, unless — just like in *One Thousand and One Nights* or at least like in *The Decameron* — to narrate and, if they have no stories to narrate, to narrate themselves? Perhaps the girls didn't have much to say, but the king's son had plenty.

---

42 He received ageless youth and deathless life.

But this delight passed as well, and then he "married the *young* girl." Let us retain that the young girl was the one whom he married, not only because she was the one who received him from the beginning and knew him better than her sisters (she had seen his still human face, we would say), but also because (as we said again) the young girl was the individual creature in the world of being, and only person with person can truly marry.

The older girls were not at all jealous, they were not yearning for a man, and this could be again understood on the basis of the archetype of being since their lot ("one as young as the other," but older than the individual creature) was to not have an independent embodiment and a precise identity. The fairytale doesn't tell us if they were tall or not, delightful or not, as it said about the first. They were thus more ethereal creatures, as determinations and general meanings are in the bosom of the archetype of being.

The honeymoon may have passed, and thus the earthly bridegroom had to come out of the palace a little. This time, all three mistresses of the house, not only his bride, but his sisters-in-law as well, told him what to do to fill his day: "The other sisters showed him the other parts of the land and told him he can walk anywhere but to avoid one place, the Valley of Tears."

Truly speaking, even if it had been called the Valley of Life, the ageless young man would not have gone there, for he had fully found that which he was looking for. And it is good to already say that, in our tale, it doesn't happen, as in all tales, that our hero (or heroine) wills with all his being to go precisely in the room or place that was forbidden. Only chance could have brought him there; still, you are tempted to believe that such chance could have never happened since he had arrived where he had to, lived as he liked, and he was guarded, with goodness and love, not only by his wife but also his airy sisters-in-law. Thus, he spent "an immemorable time," such a beautiful and deep expression that you wonder whether the creator of the tale, whoever he may have been, was not also, for a moment at least, in the kingdom of being so that he remembered the forgotten time that must reign "there."

If this fairytale were a common one, Făt-Frumos would not only begin to feel the tormenting sting to go where it had been forbidden for him, but at least—admitting that in the world of achieved being you no longer have such earthly curiosities—the story would need a completely special event, let's say a completely rare game, unseen and above any price, to attract him to the "Valley of Tears" or of Life. But the game that pushes Prince Charming there is something that cannot be more common, a simple rabbit!

How are we to understand this new strangeness of the fairytale, which is a fairytale like all fairytales and, even if it brings forward stereotypical situations from any tale comes to change their meaning, connection, and role from time to time? But, you see, it is the tale of *being,* and, even if all are the way they are in this world, in the world of fulfilled being they seem somehow inside out; as someone said, everything that is left in this world would be right there, as in a mirror; everything that is broken here is safe there, everything that is unsettled here is settled there. Thus, if totally uncommon states and events are needed for the world here, or a tremendous and unparalleled game so that the hero of the tale could accomplish his tremendous work and get in danger for it, there, in the world of being, where all things are well measured and ordered, a single changed breeze, a single extra wave on the water of the lake, or a single rabbit, as now, are sufficient to overturn a good situation.

In fact, on first sight, there was no special overturn when Făt-Frumos "hit the rabbit with his third arrow. Without noticing, he had passed into the Valley of Tears." The only thing that happens is that, while he returned with the rabbit home, Făt-Frumos felt how something rose, as a wave on the lake of conscience, something that had stayed until then well placed on "immemorable time." The fold of this thought, as an insignificant step, as a rabbit in the world of beasts, rose slowly from the forgetfulness of times, and the young man *remembered,* began to remember. This was sufficient for the world of being to tremble. For, as the tale says, all things are overturned there: here, in our world, the main thing is remembrance, while in the world of being everything must be forgetfulness, under a gentle amnesia.

Făt-Frumos comes out of gentle amnesia for a moment. Since he was in the world of being, he could not remember any banal thing but only that which, in the order of common life, is closest to being, that is, conception. He thus remembered his parents and, as the fairytale says, "he was hit suddenly by a terrible longing for his father and mother."

Something earthly, something of the order of becoming, regardless of how akin it still is to being, came to trouble the kingdom of being. The girls, his wife and his sisters in law, felt the breath of a different wind in their world. "'Unfortunate one, you passed through the Valley of Tears!' they told him utterly scared." Făt-Frumos admitted it, since, of course, there is no place for lying in the world of true being.

There's no place for return to good forgetfulness in the world of being either, as long as a single memory was awakened, with its reverberation in thought, just as being cannot remake itself just as it was if the vibration of becoming was stirred in it for a moment with its reverberation in reality.

Just as in Act V of *Faust II,* where a single bell sound of the natural world, the one from the small temple of Philemon and Baucis, brings a vast disturbance in the world of crystal, that perfectly rationalized order that the old Faust had instituted over nature, now, in the purity of being's "immemorable time," a single memory, a single impurity, seems to be sufficient to shake the entire edifice.

Except that Being is stronger than all of Faust's constructions, and it resists staining, continuing to remain in its world, immortal, somewhat cold and, in any case, boring. The only victim was *man,* who had been raised to the level of being and who no longer knew if he could be further this way or if he had to risk his un-being. Thus, he said to his companions, "I am melting because of the longing for my parents, but I cannot bring myself to leave you either." What could he do? Perhaps try to do both, he thought. "I will go to see my parents one last time, and then I'll return never to leave again." He wanted to reenter the living waters of becoming *întru* becoming, to then return to the calm waters of being. This is how he imagined it: that he can do a second time that which no one else has done even once.

"Do not leave us, our dear one," his wife and sisters in law tell him, "Your parents have not been alive for hundreds of years, and, if you go, we are afraid that you will not return." It is touching that even now, when he is about to crumble by re-immersing himself into blind flowing, they tell him gently only this: "we are afraid."[43] They encourage him, from their soul that was touched by the encounter with a human creature, to not humanize himself again. "Stay with us," they tell him. Stay with us, so in being; remain as a *homo otiosus,*[44] made eternal.

Despite the women and the horse pleading with him not to leave (the horse reappears on the scene now because it is about remaking the connection between one world and the other, which belong to him[45]), his longing for his parents was unconsolable, and this was withering him completely." What do you expect, a human offshoot cannot remain for a time out of proportion in the "immemorable time." He wants *to time.*[46] He wants the telling, reminding time and, if not, at least the turning time, any time, but he can no longer endure non-time.

Now, when the charm of forgetfulness disintegrated and when there is nothing else to do by the representatives of the world from above, the intermediary comes into play, the daimon, so the enchanted horse, who, it appears, hasn't become bored grazing in the meadows of that paradise. As any skilled mediator, he finds a way, a key, some means to do both things. But he tells Făt-Frumos, "If you won't listen, master, know that

43 The Romanian *ne temem* is gentler than "we are afraid." It suggests something close to "we are worried."

44 A peaceful, disengaged human. Latin in the original.

45 Noica's parenthetical note in the Romanian edition.

46 The Romanian verb here is *a vremui,* which comes from *vreme* ("time"). Someone who "times" would be someone who gets older together with time, who is spent just as time gets spent.

whatever happens it's your fault. I'll tell you something and if you accept my covenant,[47] I'll take you back."

His covenant. The words of this fairytale are unwavering, as in a perfect poem. By his trade, the mediator knows what a covenant is, as he also knows how to negotiate and to thus arrive at a good "covenant," according to this Romanian word of Slavic origin that means "to do equally for both." This is what he would want and what he could do as mediator: to do things *equally*, to arrange things in such a way as to be good for him and for his master for the world above and for the world below.

This Romanian horse is truly a good and skillful educator, just like the centaur Chiron, who had educated Achilles. Unfortunately, our horse didn't teach Făt-Frumos enough it seems, and, after all, Chiron had not succeeded with Achilles either; truly, no teacher has succeeded with his disciples. Such is his covenant, to use the words of the horse, that man is not given to learn everything from the wise. This is why the young man responds to the horse, "I accept gratefully." However, he will do like all disciples: he thanks and does not accept. Now, the horse teaches and educates him: "When we get to your father's palace, I'll drop you off and I'll go back, if you decide to stay even for an hour." His young master answers, "So be it." But could it be so with a man cub?

It may seem curious that such an enchanted horse, who had re-become enchanted only through the king's son and who had been body and soul with him, considered to return by himself, in case his master would not listen to him. Was it a parental or fraternal threat of the lad's wiser part? Or his half, his means, his hands, and his wings could indeed take their independence if he, the master, proved to be foolish? Who knows? In case the detachment between man's means and the man who brought them into play could be done, perhaps this detachment wants to com-

47 We chose the word "covenant" for the Romanian *tocmeală*, which Noica further explains. In Romanian, it includes the idea of negotiation. A *tocmeală* is both the negotiation that takes place between two parties and the agreement to which they arrive.

municate this in our tale: it may not be given to man to remain at the height of his aspirations. However, if his means were at the level of the aspirations (an Indian wisdom says that the means must be at the height of the purpose), then they can remain someplace in the meadows of eternity. The hero may degrade but not his means, if they were indeed good as the thought and the purpose of the hero were.

"They made their preparations": "they hugged the women (so the women embrace the horse too, not only the man[48]) and, after they said their goodbyes, left them behind sighing and with tears in their eyes." Being sighs at times too, then, or perhaps its girls. Is there in this sigh only the regret that man risked destroying himself by plunging back into the waters of life? Or is there something from the sadness of their good relative, the Evening Star from Eminescu's poem, the sadness that some creatures are not given to truly have an individual embodiment? In any case, being sighs too at times, in the ancient Romanian view, and its sigh is like one more goodness and one more smile toward our world.

Făt-Frumos returned toward our world with his wings and horse body, truly making his way back, step by step. He no longer encounters nature and its beasts, it's true; in fact, he had not really faced them even when he came, with his third trial, since he could not measure up to them, but he only passed above them. Now, he no longer needed to go over them flying, but he could pass through them in peace, as he must have done, since he had made peace with them, *întru* common being. On the other hand, the tale specifies exactly that "they arrived on the places where the realm of Scorpia was," so where the second trial had taken place, at the hour of coming.

They found there "cities instead. The forests had changed into plains." Years and centuries had passed, and history brought civilization with it, our folkloric fairytale tells us. It's true that the tale doesn't get too scared by the many cities that have been raised in the meantime, by the transformation of the world into

48 Noica's parenthetical note.

a world of cities, as it doesn't show any open worry toward the vast deforestations that had happened to obtain plains, which were fertile at the beginning but were more and more devastating of nature. We now know well that the forests of Thrace, once they disappeared, transformed the fruitful land of Greece into a naked stone, good for goats only, because of lack of rain; we know just as well that the mad forest of Teleorman[49] disappeared, the forest around which this Wallachian story may have been born. But the tale doesn't know it or has the discretion not to say it.

What this folkloric fairytale knows, though, and it knows with certainty, is what the mind of man discovered today, through scientific means of course, and this is the fact that time flows in a way in one part of the world, let's say of the cosmos, and in a different way in another part. Without going into science fiction, the fairytale calmly narrates how Făt-Frumos, when he arrived at this stage of his return, "asked around about Scorpia and her house, but they told him that their grandparents heard such stories from their ancestors."

This is why people "laughed at him (when he told them what he knew from the past[50]), and thought he was crazy." Perhaps this is how those who may return once from the cosmos would wander with their minds, without realizing that their time had not been truly theirs; and one of them may get upset, just like Făt-Frumos now, and "without his noticing, his beard and hair turned white."

It's true, science says that those left behind would get older, while the flyers through cosmos would remain unbelievably younger. But who knows if, once they returned after years and years in their time from another time, they would not suddenly get older, as Făt-Frumos now, growing a beard and having their hair whiten all of a sudden? The fairytale may not tell a lie, even in this case.

49 A southern region of Romania.
50 Noica's parenthetical note in the Romanian edition.

Just like Scorpia, through whose realm Făt-Frumos passed, Gheonoaia, her blood sister, had not left traces in the world. "He arrived at the land of Gheonoaia, where he asked the same questions that he asked in the land of Scorpia, and he received similar answers." Of course, the tale says, Făt-Frumos "was baffled" how so many things had changed, just in a few days, as it seemed to him. However, although he was getting upset because of the errors of those from the re-found world, he could have indeed realized that much more time had passed if he had a mirror with him, to see that he had now "a white beard, all the way to his waist." He could have realized even without a mirror since "his legs were weak and trembled" at the moment when he was about to arrive in his father's kingdom.

What waited for him there? "Different people, new cities, and the old ones were so changed that he could no longer recognize them… Finally, he arrived at the palace of his birth," and thus the loop was closed: man returned to his original place and, in a sense, the cycle of his destiny is over.

But he doesn't know it yet; the horse knows it, who, immediately after Făt-Frumos arrived in the places where he was born and dismounted him, no longer waited to see what his master said, the young man from before, and didn't even mention the condition, "if you remained even for an hour," but, realizing from the beginning that his master ended the cycle of his destiny, kissed his hand (remember this, listeners of the tale, what the horse does: he kisses his hand) and told him, "Be well, master, I'll now return to where we came from."

He barely adds, aside, "If you want to come, get back in the saddle and let's go!" But the horse knew well why he kissed his hand, since he didn't kiss it out of the joy that they returned on the land of death. Thus, the moment his master told him, "Go in peace, for I also hope to return soon," he immediately started back toward eternity, "as fast as an arrow." What can you say before this seeming unfaithfulness of the horse, unless that the means leave us too when we leave them?

There is a question: what was in the mind of the young lad, now old as he was, when he said that he also hoped to return "soon," lagging though in the world from which there was no return even with the enchanted horse, if he lingered more than a moment, an hour? Did he want to say, I will return to being by the memory that I now regained? I will return to being by the entrance in non-being?

We don't know, and the tale doesn't give us clues. But this is how man speaks at times, in his foolishness ("I'll go back sometime"), and Făt-Frumos, the old Făt-Frumos, said it from the tips of his lips, and then he truly entered in the Valley of Tears. He had seen its overturned model in the world of being, where he hunted his rabbit. Now, "when he saw the abandoned castle with wild plants and weeds all over it, he sighed and, with tears in his eyes, tried to remember the glory days of his childhood, the rooms and halls filled with light."

This is all he gained now, memory, in the place of "immemorable time." But if he no longer liked forgotten time, memory is no longer good either but rather very bitter. It was the memory of becoming *întru* becoming, that vain evocation of what was and will no longer be, and not the evocation — we'll say beyond the tale, but who knows if not under its influence — that carries man toward knowledge and enriches him, for it brings back to his mind that which he contemplated some other time, as the fairytale narrator and myths from Antiquity, Plato, used to say.[51]

The son descends now in remembrance, "looking in every room and corner that reminded him of the past"; he descends into thought, and he descends properly speaking since "he went down to the cellar, which had its entrance occluded by the rubble." Only there, in the occluded cellars of the real and of thought, could he still find, deeply buried, his past life. Devouring time had caught him in its whirlwind by now, and it almost blinded him, as it blinded Faust in his later years, and thus he could only see if he lifted "his eyelids with his fingers."

51 Noica refers most likely to the charioteer allegory in the *Phaedros* (246a–254e), where the soul of a human being, prior to birth, travels in the world of ideas and perceives them.

And what did he see? What kingly trace did he see? A "rumbling throne"; perhaps not even a kingly throne but a simple peasant trunk.

There was something from the past life. But it had to be something that belonged to him, only to him, for which he had come there. He opened the throne and found nothing at the beginning; but in the small box from inside the trunk, so in the small trunk inside the trunk, well hidden, or perhaps deeply buried, there was his ultimate intimacy, his death. "Welcome! If you had been late just a tad longer, I would have died myself"

Was it only that she waited for him? Or did he actually look for her too? Perhaps it was her that he looked for when he left the world of being, even though he didn't know it well for he longed to see his parents and, with them, to recover his world and so his measure, his limit, his consummation. For she was *his* death, not general Death, with her scythe, who comes to cut all life on earth.

The death that was enclosed here couldn't be the usual, spectral one, which is untouchable by man. It couldn't be a more concrete death either, which appears in Creangă's story,[52] for example, the death that Ivan thrusts into his bag first, having the God-given gift to thrust in there whoever he wanted, and the second death he throws into his coffin, and so nobody else dies and the plans of the good God are hampered.

The death from this fairytale, who was about to die, had not precluded the rest of the world to continue dying, according to natural laws: Făt-Frumos's parents, Gheonoaia, Scorpia, their worlds, and the entire world since them until this time have all died. Death has a single name and can only be one, but she has endlessly many faces according to this Romanian tale.

Just like being, which in the Romanian view of the world is not a single and massive general nature, it doesn't have a single level of subsistence nor a single face (but, at the most, a single

52 In Creangă's story *Ivan Turbincă*, the main character is a Russian soldier who is able to put anything in his bag at his command. Ivan commands death to go in there, and so people stop dying.

model and archetype), death belongs to each and is the measure of each. The one here, for example, "had shriveled so much that she was bent like a hook in the small chest." However, she still has the strength to slap the decrepit Făt-Frumos.

But why does she slap him? Why doesn't she draw him slowly, with her hook, toward nonbeing, as it happened to everyone else, now when he fell by himself under her sovereignty? She slapped him, perhaps, because this man had had the impertinence to come out of his condition as man, transcending pure becoming *întru* becoming. An act of violence was necessary, so that the rest of being that remained in him be transformed into smithereens and smoke, entering the order of nonbeing.

Death is individual, not generic; it is of each one. It doesn't cut lives one after the other, but it ends the life of each according to the measure of his life. It flaps one, it caresses another, and it transfigures another as it transfigured Johann Sebastian Bach, the organ player.

When the memory was aroused in him and when the chamber of his memories was disturbed, Făt-Frumos had understood that a measure must be given to him as well. In a way, the girls of Being had understood it also, and they let him go. They didn't have the cruelty to punish their chosen one with eternal life and with its ugliness.[53] For there, in the world of being, there is a certain world of the pure general, in which people have no dwelling.

There may be other creatures, other rational beings in cosmos, who stay as lichens or moss, as a scholar of our days imagined, and have who knows what delights, experiences, and knowledge that are foreign to us. We, however, are just like in the world of this fairytale. Even if we come out of our condition and delay too long in the indetermination of eternity, a curse seems to reach us, that folkloric curse: "May he know no rest, / For him dinner may be no dinner, / Sleep may be no sleep, / Home may be no home, / And may he care without knowing what he cares about." This is how we would be there: we would

53 Ugliness should be understood here in the sense of boredom.

resent that we care, in the sense that something is heavy on us and makes us think, but this something is nothing; eternalized nothingness.

Trees do not grow to the sky, and people's lives give themselves borders from the inside; they border themselves even when they penetrate and are about to remain in the undecidedness of eternity.[54] There is fulfilment without eternalization. The archetype of being remains, but its embodiments pass. It is a liar the one who doesn't believe it.[55]

The narrator mounts a saddle,[56] going back without an enchanted horse, into the world of Reminiscence, from which an ancient thinker extracted its myths, while this narrator extracted his tales from folklore.

The analysis of the *Evening Star* suggested an enrichment to the ontological model, seeing that it is not the inferior term only, the individual, that stays under vicissitudes, but also the general itself, and highlighting a splendid opposition between worlds, between the misery of the general and the serenity of the individual. Now, the fairytale "Ageless Youth" comes to enrich the ontological model with a new and unexpected lesson, that determinations, so the middle term, can also stay under vicissitudes.

In appearance, determinations shouldn't have autonomy since everything is reduced to the couple individual-general and to its balance or unbalance. Aren't determinations simple natural manifestations of the individual, on the one hand, chaotic at the beginning, and of the general, on the other hand, which is steadfast in order? What kind of independence could the de-

---

54 Untranslatable play of words: "border" translates *hotar,* while "undecidedness," *nehotărâre.* To be undecided is to have no borders, no limits: a limit makes a decision.

55 This clause appears often at the end of Romanian fairytales, where the "testament" for the truth of the story is expressed through this statement: it is a liar the one who doesn't believe it.

56 Another reference to a usual way of ending fairytales.

terminations of a nature, be it individual or general, have apart from that nature itself?

The fairytale "Ageless Youth" came to show that there can be an individual nature, there can be a good balance between it and a general nature, without determinations existing in a full sense. What impulse does this Romanian tale give then to thinking? It teaches it to see that there can be a perfect balance between individual and general — that Făt-Frumos and the girls of Being can get married — but this marriage may not take place fully *întru* being, because being, according to its model, needs something else, let's say offspring, children. It needs determinations — good, full, and active determinations. They do not appear, though, in the world there, or they appear only in the shape of hunting for a rabbit, which is able, if it escapes from two arrows, to bring together with the third the slipping of Făt-Frumos into the Valley of Crying, so to awake the conscience of ugliness into a world in which nothing happens.

But wasn't the world above, after all, precisely the world that man and everything that is a living creature crave? Wasn't this the world of "being"?

It was, of course. But it was only the world of being without existence. Being, life, and death require certain embodiments, on the basis of certain determinations, and when they are not clear, so they no longer have a name and become anonymous, being enters the boredom of anonymity as well.

The being of things, though, has names: they are their *archai,* every time different ones, but the same in terms of model. The Romanian fairytale brings us to the Romanian thought of being as archetype, a thought that Eminescu carried with him, Eminescu who seemed to have come from the same world of Reminiscence from which the fairytale had descended.

V

The Archai

Rethinking the Supreme Principles

In the Romanian view, it is not only the world of the individual that is subject to adversities, but also the world of the general. If there were such a thing as a cosmic mind and a demiurge of the universe, together with its company of god-stars as portrayed by Eminescu's poem, they would show through one or the other, like the Evening Star, how much space there is for disorientation in the world of the general. If, similarly, there were a paradise as portrayed in the story *Ageless Youth,* the human being would not need to be chased out of it but would leave on its own.

Absolute reason and absolute nature haven't responded to the Romanian sentiment of being. The latter aims towards an animated reason, as requested by a nature with more concrete determinations. After all, modern thinking has abandoned absolute generals. Rather, when it comes to reason and nature, *they had to be reconsidered and needed to acquire* — as the Romanian sentiment of being implicitly required — *modified aspects, even if they were not and must not be completely abandoned.*

Nature, as it was understood in the past, proved itself increasingly and comprehensively wrong, leading to today's threat that is hanging above it. As an explanatory principle, nature was, at first, a model of continuity. In ancient times and then in the

Middle Ages, the belief was that nature does not make jumps. Later we saw that nature *does* make jumps; that it is discreet or discontinuous, such that, from biological mutations to quants in physics, everything now invalidates nature as a model or supreme principle of continuity.

One might say that, along with being discontinuous, nature might be invoked as explanatory and supreme principle against which to evaluate the processes and phenomena of reality. However, science itself found in nature not just discontinuity but something more important that prevents its use as a model: uncertainty. The notion that nature never makes a mistake has long been abandoned. Nature not only makes mistakes, but it seems to register more failures than successes, such that one could speak about nature's naiveté on all sorts of levels: the naiveté of putting out species that don't make it; the naiveté of seeking fecundation through the absurd path of spreading dandelion seeds (and others) in all directions; the naiveté of making the mouth both a feeding organ and a speaking organ ("tongue" means two things); or, if we can quote Hegel's crude thoughts, the naiveté of making the same organ for urination and procreation.

At least, as an explanatory principle, nature could show how to depart from simple elements and arrive at something complex through evolution, and in general, it could show, and not mechanically, that the simple precedes the complex. Many thinkers and scientists approached nature with this assumption, not to mention writers and ideologists like Rousseau[1] and his whole generation. But nature did not keep its promise in this regard either. A deep knowledge of nature and its fundamental processes has shown that the simple does not precede the complex, but the other way around. One example is provided by organisms in movement which originally moved in a spiral fashion, not a straight line, which became a particular case of spiral movement. I won't delve into the issues and logical vicis-

1 Jean Jacques Rousseau (1712–78), French philosopher, influential figure of the Enlightenment.

situdes raised by the simple elements of nature, like the cell or the atom, issues that proved to be extraordinarily complex.

In any case, more surprising that nature's weakening as an explanatory principle is its questioning by its own product, man. Already man can destroy parts of external nature, but he can also garden it to his will, reestablish[2] it as he wishes, at least in part.

When one sees so many biologists and naturalists defending nature with all sorts of arguments, including esthetic ones, stating that nature with all its species and subspecies should survive, one might think they do this out of love and understanding towards nature. In reality, the majority of their arguments could be reduced to "Polluting and destroying nature are not good for *man*."

In fact, it is the animality inside man that sometimes needs nature and sometimes doesn't. That is why nature, the great principle of old times, is only tolerated on Earth. There will be only so much external nature as man will desire or will need. If making the earth green suits man, he will turn the planet green; if laying pavement on the Earth's crust suits him (when he will discover photosynthesis), that is what he will do.

This is then what happened with nature considered as supreme principle, both for knowledge and the affirmation of being. We're left with the second principle, *logos,* or reason, which has also been invoked as supreme principle that cannot be replaced, even when it seems deficient. Today it is clear that *logos* is being questioned, as it was in the time of the sophists. Only today, reason (from Hegelian and Marxist perspectives, the intellect) endangered itself through its own deepened exercise, and not through cunning and empty talent as was the case of the sophists.

Here is an example of questioning *logos* as supreme principle, still an unreplaceable value. Just as during Kant's time, reason was summoned by the tribunal of reason itself. Around 1900s,

2 The Romanian term here is *reînființa,* so "give-being-again." The idea is that man would reestablish the being of nature on his own criteria.

this time disguised as mathematical logic, reason summoned reason embodied in its most confident of disciplines, mathematics, and it failed to see its ultimate justification.

However, characteristically for our times, no one became intimidated by this, on the contrary. Kant and his four antinomies of reason had stirred such an indescribable emotion among the intellectuals of his time who saw an important moral lesson for man in this tragedy suffered by reason, as did Kant himself who then wrote *Critique of Practical Reason*. Later, we had Hegel and Marx saying there are not only four antinomies but an infinite number and that reason "falls into" antinomies to find itself again as reason. On the other hand, today's world of science did not see the paradoxes of logic as dramatic or its own observed limits for that matter. On the contrary, it saw it as a positive because, if all things were logically explained, then sciences could be taken over by machines. Thus, this is where the weakening of the second supreme principle, the *logos*, got us.

But if the supreme principles no longer satisfy us, what can explain being if not nature and reason in a more moderated and animated view expressed by the Romanian philosophical sensitivity.

Entities, Spirits, Daimons

It is well known that Heraclitus, having to host his friends in his kitchen, told them something to the effect, "No worries, there are gods even in the kitchen."[3]

Being is not sacred, if we understand the sacred as absolute. On the contrary, being is precarious, since something general doesn't exist without determinations and without an individual

3 Noica paraphrases Aristotle, who says in *Parts of Animals*, "Every realm of nature is marvellous: and as Heraclitus, when the strangers who came to visit him found him warming himself at the furnace in the kitchen and hesitated to go in, is reported to have bidden them not to be afraid to enter, as even in that kitchen divinities were present, so we should venture on the study of every kind of animal without distaste" (645a17–22).

embodiment, neither does something individual without determinations and an anchoring in the general, and neither yet do empty determinations without an individual reality that can produce them and a general one to hold them together, so there isn't just "the shadow of a dream"; even more, it is precarious since one of the three terms can still be missing, as it can also be in deficiency or in excess.

Still, all three elements are required along with their adequate harmony for being to exist. Thus, it is explainable why being as such can't be found just about anywhere (traditional ontology looked for it in the skies), but it is equally explainable that being can be found just about everywhere when a good harmony exists among the three terms.

What is the face taken by being in this case? Being takes the face of a reality that cannot be seen with the naked eye, nor with the telescope. When Cremonini, the Aristotelian philosopher from Padova, was invited by his friend Galilei to look through the telescope to convince himself that the moon was not as perfect and incorruptible as Aristotle had said, he refused, saying that he knew very well that the moon was perfect. In reality, the telescope and the naked eye were needed to see the moon and many other things, but Cremonini embarrassed himself in history. Plato on the other hand, did not embarrass himself when he told Antisthenes, who could see the horse but not the Idea of a horse, that he had eyes to see the horse but didn't have eyes for the Idea.[4] Regardless of how things are with Plato, it is a fact that certain realities and everything we could call being can be seen not by the common eye, the microscope, or the telescope, but by a different eye.

What is this being that cannot be seen with the common eye? Is it maybe the great being we have been told about for so long? No, because this great being has died — it was, in fact, dead from the beginning: it was only what we didn't know to say about

4 This is a reference to the Aristotelian commentator Simplicius who mentions such a dialogue between Plato and Antisthenes in his commentary on Aristotle's *Categories* (208.28–32).

it. As we have seen, nature as supreme principle was debated, as was reason, by those who don't know the difference between reason (dialectic) and intellect (logic).

What principles then have replaced the ones invalidated? Could they be the other gods, those from Heraclitus's kitchen?

They cannot be seen by the common eye either. "The spirit of the times," for example, that of the language, of the community, or of a place cannot be seen with a telescope. (One could say that Cremonini had a philosophical instinct, but one that is applied in reverse in the field of natural sciences.) Relationships of production or social-historical formations cannot be seen with the common eye. No species could be seen by the scientist with his common eye although he thinks it is real.

The same thing could be said about structures of any kind — they cannot be seen. And although they are not only formal, they not only cannot be seen, but they also cannot be formalized completely, like the object of mathematics. Thought often has other realities in front of it. Or rather, it sees something else in the same realities considered by sciences.

We must have the audacity to name the realities seen as such with the name always given to them: entities. In Romanian thought, Athanase Joja knew how to reposition, from a Marxist perspective, the eternal problem of philosophy — the "abstract entities." In their own ways, all sciences rise to the level of abstract entities, such as the number in mathematics, the code in genetics, the family, the genus or the species in biology, or the structures in chemistry (think of Kekulé's[5] striking hexagon for instance), not to mention the abstract entities invoked by the humanist sciences. However, from the perspective of this model of being, it is the task of thinking to consider those entities that acquire the function of the third element in the model, the general. Thus, the entities become, as we shall soon see, concrete universals.

Indeed, abstract entities in sciences tend too often to be effectively "abstract." In this sense, one could think that any ab-

5 Friedrich August Kékulé (1829–96), German organic chemist.

straction in science could also be considered an abstract entity. The word "entity" contains *ens,* and an entity, no matter how abstract, possesses a defined boundary, a consistency, a given nature. Thus, the numbers theory in mathematics does not represent an abstract entity, but the number does. The theory of evolution is not an abstract entity, but the species that evolves is. In general, an "-ism" cannot be regarded as an entity.

If we return now to the spirit, we realize even more strongly what deserves to be called an abstract entity and how it can transition into a concrete universal. What Hegel called spirit for instance, as in the spirit of a community, the Romanian speech called it "breath." The entire "Romanian breath" we say today to refer to an entity that must be considered abstract only to the degree it does not possess anything from the common concrete. We can also talk about the breath of a language, a culture, or a civilization — breath, not soul as Spengler would have wanted.

Our ancient language had another term that would be even more appropriate for spirit than "breath," *dihanie*[6] which comes from *duh,* which is "spirit." In the sixteenth century, one could find the expression "the entire Romanian *daimon,*" meaning all the Romanian spirit. We mention the term daimon only to make even more suggestive the discussion about entities and breaths.

Entities and breaths are not without *us,* that is without individual realities of any order (the number does not exist without numbers, no matter how general), but at the same time we cannot *be* without them. The French language speaker, for example, knows that he stands under a spirit that asks him to use a certain order in his speech, to place accents only on the last syllable, to sing the words, and to roll the *r* a certain way. Who could claim that the spirit of French language has an independent existence? But, without being independent of us speakers, a language is like a daimon, toying with the one caught in it. The Romanian language rejected the Italian expressions proposed by Heliade

6 Noica explains the word *dihanie* in the text, so we will not do it here. From now on, whenever he uses *dihanie,* the English version will have "daimon."

Rădulescu[7] despite the two languages being related; it also rejected being enriched with words of Slavic origin, although its lexicon contains a large percentage of Slavic words; instead, in the nineteenth century when languages acquired all kinds of neologisms, it chose to borrow words from French (with a Latin root in almost every new word). So today, when we count the words in our language, over thirty percent of them have a French–Latin origin.

But languages and communities are only one kind of breaths. Many other entities can, from their abstract, get close to a broader form of concrete, becoming daimons. There are objects of speech or thought that initially do not appear to be entities but who end up becoming true breaths. A high school class, for example, is first an administrative structure. But when later the former students invoke it — "junior year" from back then at such and such high school — doesn't it start to have something of an entity, to acquire its own spirit, like a breath that blows over and through those youth?

Here we have an example of how a high school class can become a true daimon, from entity and then from breath. An experiment was conducted a while ago in our country: the top students from all over the country were gathered in one class of "top performers." What were the outcomes of this experiment? A "class" formed in the vivid sense of the word, one where some students were submissive and others were troublemakers; some were active intelligences, while others were lazy intelligences; top performers and bottom dwellers, or close. The top performers organized themselves and became one class. The spirit of a class marked those students, or one could say this spirit bit their minds and hearts, turning them into what was fit for it. We don't want to say it turned them into "what it wanted" because we would fall into who knows what objective idealism.

If this seems like a minor example, let's choose one with an incontestable scientific dignity: the number. A mathematician

7 Ion Heliade Rădulescu (1802–72), Romanian poet and essayist. He advocated for the introduction of Italian neologisms in Romanian.

doesn't philosophize with the number, and he is not interested if you name his work instrument an abstract entity. However, Pythagoras and his disciples philosophized the number. For them, whole numbers and natural numbers were entities, strange, abstract entities that made each reality have its own constitutive number. The mathematicians focused on their specialty and showed, over centuries, many other facets of a number beyond that of being natural, that is, its negative aspect, its rational aspect in fractions, its irrational aspect with the "real" number, its imaginary aspect with complex numbers. With these structures, we didn't need a contemporary Pythagoras to philosophize the number, because the number philosophized itself in our scientific culture.

Indeed, this culture claimed the mastery of the number over reality (first in astronomy, then in physics, chemistry, biology, and social sciences, if we want to maintain the positivistic scheme), and one could clearly see how this abstract entity, the number, became a breath and a spirit that permeates almost everything, as it seems. If one dares to reprise the image of the daimon[8] and take it to the end, one could say that it revealed one of its claws, the negative, and then another, the rational, and then another, the irrational, and then the most penetrating of all, the imaginary; and the daimon then thrusted all these claws in the real. And its grasp was so strong that a great mathematician like Euler said about just one trigonometric equation that carried the imaginary number that it was simply "the diagram of truth."

What must be said beyond these examples and formulas that are too plastic to be remembered is that abstract entities can do very concrete work in the real. That is the reason why we aspire toward them, as instances that can replace and have always replaced the lazy gods of philosophical thought. As was the case for the number, the contemporary man's philosophical reflection could often occur outside of the field of philosophy. Thus, even today's technology led to the abstract entities incor-

8 Here, "daimon" in the sense of wild spirit, wild beast.

porated like the cybernetic systems or the systems described by the systems theory itself, which could be described as a theory of abstract entities.

Nevertheless, we must return to such gods in order to speak about being. We may see that they acquire a well-defined shape and a concrete description present in Eminescu's archai. These minor gods are like the general in the model of being or like the horizon in which the preposition întru makes an opening. These gods are not only ephemeral, but they may not exist at all. But even then, if they are well invoked, they are the ones that bring being into the world.

Eminescu's *Archai*

For the minor gods that we reminded, Eminescu gave various drafts in several of his manuscripts. They seemed to lead either to a short, independent philosophical work or, as it was judged more probable, to a philosophical introduction to a great story that remained unfinished, *The Avatars of Pharaoh Tla,* according to the title given by G. Călinescu.[9]

9 Noica's note in the Romanian edition: Almost all of these fragments were signaled and highlighted, on the philosophical level, beginning with the first years of the research of the manuscripts until today. Thus, in the 1905 edition Ion Scurtu published the philosophical fragment *Archaeus,* from manuscript 2269, 18–39. Ion Rădulescu-Pogoneanu asked for its critical exam in "Kant and Eminescu," *Convorbiri Literare* 40 (1906): 68. George Călinescu, a literary critic, studied it in detail in *The Work of Eminescu,* Vol. 3 (Bucharest, 1965). Then, later, in the volume Mihai Eminescu, *Proza literară* [*Literary Prose*], eds. Eugen Simion and Flora Suteu (Bucharest, 1964), 205–15, the fragment appears with the title *Archaeus* after it was interestingly commented in the Introduction, pp. XLIIff. Prior drafts exist in ms. 2287, 70–75, and in the Perpessicius edition (Vol. I, p. 358), which reminds of the "German pagination, on related reasons, in the ms. 2262, 42," which is in fact, he says, "the translation in German of the end of the *Archaeus,*" which makes him situate the writing of the fragment "during the time of preparing for the doctorate and of interpreting Kant," so around 1874.

He notices that this "fragment is more evolved conceptually and creates a special element"[10] and I find it completely appropriate. Noticing, in passing, that the critic's indication that the idea of *archē* appears in Paracelsus and in Van Helmont, and it can remind of the principle of identity, prototype of every individual, about which Edgar Poe spoke, let us go deeper here as well[11] into this notion. I will do so on the basis of the same text from manuscript 2268, which the commentators do not usually use, since they rather focus on the fragment from manuscript 2269.

"But before telling me about king Tla, I would like you to tell me what you understand by Archaeus, whose name you mentioned so many times this evening?"

"My dear... I told you about the manuscript from the drawer. You will accept that the entire comedy would not have taken place [...] if that insignificant hundred-year-old manuscript were not in the back of the drawer. How much richness [...] in just a few soiled pages in which Archaeus dwelt" — "A living icon of life," Eminescu said in some other work.

"Well, consider life as comedy: who arranges it? Consider man as a machine: who supports it? Consider nature as background: who paints it? Then, don't forget that the paper was necessary only to fixate Archaeus. If you take away the manuscript, does he no longer exist? Of course he does. What was him? A nothing, a possibility... But imagine now that in the middle of the representation, a wall falls, an actor breaks his head, another forgets his role... here's an offended Archaeus, and you feel as if you offended him. Why do you feel? Because that nothing is also in you, and what is insulted on the stage is also insulted in you. Nevertheless, he could have remained in the drawer for thousands of years, and his body of paper could have rotted, you may

10 George Călinescu, *Opera lui Eminescu* [*Eminescu's Work*] (Bucharest: Cultura Naţională, 1935), 3:145.

11 Noica's note in the Romanian edition: As in Constantin Noica, *Eminescu sau gânduri despre omul deplin al culturii româneşti* [*Eminescu or Thoughts about the Complete Man of Romanian Culture*] (Bucharest: Eminescu Press, 1975), 155ff.

have not been born and participate in the number of those that never were… well, existence was still possible because it is. It would have existed as an idea, as a comedy received, but whose manuscript was lost and about which no one knows anything, even if it existed, and even if it exists in the brain of nature."[12]

"Therefore, you were, you are, and you will always be."

We consider that this passage, more than the others, even if it is not usually employed by commentators, better renders the originality of Eminescu's thought regarding a theme that initially seemed to have been merely borrowed. The way he conceives it, the *archē* is a structure or a batch of structured possibilities which are to pass into the bosom of reality, if reality offers favorable conditions for its realization. What deserves to be underlined here is its firmness to be in a certain way, and only in that way.

We revealed the condition of the general above; the Evening Star belonged to its category, and now we can say that Eminescu's *archai* also belong to it, regardless of how little glorious they may seem in comparison with the former. When interpreting *The Evening Star,* we showed how there can exist, or rather subsist, a kind of structures without existence, which appear in reality all of a sudden, perfectly organized, if the conditions for their appearance are created, proving thus that they are not simple improvisations of reality. This is how those species were — literally, species of creatures that are born if the climate of Terra is slightly changed, in one or the other direction. With their perfect organization, they cannot fail to surprise anyone who pays attention to their sudden apparition in the bosom of reality. Similarly, in a different example perhaps less convincing than the one with the species of creatures that spring into reality but still connected with certain "archai," the artistic personalities or the geniuses that are capable to model large groups of

12 Noica's note in the Romanian edition: In the main fragment (see the Simion-Suteu edition), it was written: "Still, there are moments in life when these three elements of our mind (time, space, causality, Noica's note), these drawers in which we put a world, disappear for a moment…"

humanity also come to life by chance, at an hour of crisis of the spirit. Would there be a universal reason, a brain of nature, in which all of these have a kind of subsistence?

There can't be such a thing, not even in Eminescu's view, but there can, rather, be an inner structure, a rational intimacy, that deeper core of every thing, one that would bring the founders into reality; or, if it cannot do this, one that is doomed to remain in the ontological zone that we must name, together with Eminescu, the world of the *archai*. The strength that our thinker and poet sees in these *archai* is underlined by the fact that he dares to speak about the "offense" of an *archē* as if it would be about a moral person. In reality, this language only wants to show how well structured the *archē* appears to him, such that the smallest deviation could be experienced as a true injury of a prototype.

In this sense, it is a fact that from the moment in which we became aware of the presence of the *archai,* either in act or in their waiting zone, we realize how many deviations are in our world and how many we ourselves commit. A bad engagement in life, an erroneous step in humanity's progress of civilization, an apparent victory which crushes man — as some of the victories of today's society in the West — all of these represent offenses to a known or unknown *archē*. Engagement in life must be essential, not accidental and on the basis of man's deeper necessity, not of an arbitrary approach. The progress of civilization must be obtained under human control so that it doesn't turn against man, and man's victories must raise him up to order, not to the profanity of historical disorder.

We could emphasize here as well that Eminescu was saddened, in a way, by the strength of this deeper rationality of the *archai,* which created so many occasions of unhappiness for our world due to its incapacity to obtain the full realization of the *archē* and due to the offense that it brought to it. However, going beyond the poet's sorrows when faced with the consequences of his rational view, as everything that belongs to the Romanian sentiment of being, we can now see in Eminescu's *archai* precisely the principles of being, those good spirits that we were talking about and that institute being in the world when the world can offer them favorable occasions. The being of things, the being of the existent, which ontology searches — what *is* truly in the world? — receives, with the *archai,* a conceptual answer that is solidary with everything that we revealed in the unfolding of the Romanian sentiment of being, from the question about what is until the possible ontological model.

VI

The Serenity of Being from a Romanian Perspective

Our culture had three great thinkers who asked the question of being in the past: language itself,[1] a poet, and a sculptor.

The problem of being has two facets. One is darker, having to do with the difficulty of the things on earth and in the heaven of generalities to obtain being; the other is brighter, being contemplated in its universality. Language and Eminescu gave us the first facet. Still language and, surprisingly, the sculptor Brâncuşi[2] will show us the bright facet.

On the above pages, we tried to describe, according to the Romanian thought of the past, the darker side of being, more agitated by attempts and unrest, which is also the side of its knowledge, more filled with perplexities. In the first chapter, we saw how a certain horizon of being catches contour from the usual formulas of the question but even better from the less usual formulas that Romanian language brings into play.

We then saw how Romanian modulations of being emerge, which are born from questions and inquiries, a kind of situations or hypostases of being, which, without rendering it exactly,

1 Noica truly refers to language as a great thinker, in a figurative sense, of course.

2 Constantin Brâncuşi (1876–1957).

portray it as some of its snapshots: being as *it was not to be,* as *it was about to be,* as *it may well be to be,* as *it would be to be, it is to be,* and finally, *it was to be.*

In the third chapter, we saw how, from all of these signs and gleams of being in the world, a sentiment of being is born regarding the world of real creatures, giving into the momentary individual realities the chance to be or, at least, to open ontological fields, as just as many flickers of being.

We further saw how we can organize all these searches of things as well as of their knowledge into a structure, a sort of archetype or model of being, which may be fulfilled, but may also not bring being to light, under the darkness of the world of the individual or of the light of *The Evening Star* or under the blind day of unfulfillments, as in *Ageless Youth.*

We also saw, in the fifth chapter, how all of these things found a condensation in Eminescu's *archai,* which emerged as good spirits to express the way in which the world, from its darkness, still rises toward being.

In the science of being, there was usual no discussion about this being that raises from below, searching to form itself from the uncertainties and smallness of things, following a model, and being fulfilled at times under the sign of principles of organizations that Eminescu baptized *archai.* European thinkers of the past who practiced the science of being had no pity on the world below as original Romanian thinking did. They generally invoked a being from above, sure of itself and undefiled by generation and corruption, one that was fully provided with luminosity but could only throw in the shadow and, at times, in nonbeing everything that was under it. Such a being seemed to come to scold the realities of the world — realities which it had crushed — because they could not raise up to it, just as in our legends the Mother of the Forest scolds the trees because they are crooked and gnarled. Almost every ontological view from the past, the medieval view or the view of Christian Wolff (1679–1754),[3] transformed being into a Mother of the forest for

3 Christian Wolff (1679–1754), German philosopher.

the things below. Man's thought hasn't always had the courage to undertake a science of being for the realities of this world, not to say that being is "somewhere else" or at least "something else"; thus, the old Romanian view of being, which we seem to be able to detach from the treasures of language and from Eminescu's thinking, emphasizes an original note in the thought about being.

However, since we talked about the being of the real world with its darkness, what we described so far is the darker face of being. Being, in itself, is not yet at play with the joy that it can give. In any case, Eminescu didn't think of it under the sign of joy only. There is a double nature-as-thinker in him, with one face that sent him irrepressibly to ultimate problems, where there is place only for the elegy of great poems, and a face turned toward the real world, which awoke in him the interest for the concrete, for history, language and languages, the economic and dramatic realities of people's live, and even statistics. However, just as he couldn't find the joy of being in the boundlessness of the world, he couldn't find it within its boundaries either from which he struggled to extract it with his Evening Stars and *archai*.

In this sense, Eminescu continues the line from Neagoe's *Teachings,*[4] the chroniclers, and Cantemir's *Divan,*[5] where hearts pendulate between the spirit of the Psalter, invoked sincerely or conventionally, and the daring breath of human affirmations, marked as well by the precarity of everything human.

Someone brought joy, however. It was the sculptor of flight and of essences, Brâncuși. He himself used to say, with the boldness of simplicity, that he wanted to bring joy to people. He didn't give it a different name, but it is clear today, contemplating his work, that it was the joy of *settling into being*. Brâncuși describes *that which is durable,* even when he creates portraits of real beings, because he inscribes their face among general essences.

4 Neagoe Basarab (1459–1521), *Învățăturile lui Neagoe Basarab către fiul său Teodosie* [*The Teachings of Neagoe Basarab to His Son Theodosie*], one of the earliest Romanian literary works, where Neagoe Basarab writes on various subjects such as philosophy, diplomacy, morals, and ethics.

5 Dimitrie Cantemir (1673–1723), whom Noica mentioned before.

Everything that was dark and difficult for others becomes simple and has joy for him. In his work, there is a splendid "you wouldn't look for me if you haven't already found me."[6] However, instead of presenting, like Pascal, a certain agony until the end of the world, for him it becomes a jubilation which doesn't belong to faith — it was precisely faith that saddened the other one — nor does it have to do with an evasion from the world but rather with good establishment within being, together with all the things of the world.

On first sight, Brâncuşi's work may arouse worries. Hasn't he placed nature and its creatures in flowing? Everything has become disparate in an art like his, which is no longer representative but wants not to be abstract either, but superiorly presentative. Every thing has become something else. Miss Pogany is not Miss Pogany, the bird is not a bird, the kiss is not a kiss. A spectator's very way of registering and his senses become something else before this work. When you see a sculpture by Brâncuşi, the greatest suffering is that you cannot caress it, coming out of the distance and instantaneousness of sight to pass into the closeness and gentle gliding of touch. For the ancients, the first of the senses and the one that reappears in all other four is touch. *Sight is touch,* as Eminescu also says in one of his notes.

Doing so, though, so deforming things and our own sensibility of spectators, a sculptor worries you and, at the same time, tames you and models or tames the world. Things have come close to you, just as the sculptor seemed to bring them to him, or they merged and entered gliding in a different becoming than the one of passing and losing. It is like in our preposition, *întru,* and in the situation described by "to be *întru,*" where distance has no place between that which is something and the thing *în-*

6 Noica alludes here to the problematic of the Meno, where we encounter Meno's paradox: how can we search for something about which we do not know anything at all? See a discussion on this in Octavian Gabor, "Constantin Noica's 'Becoming Within Being' and 'Meno's Paradox,'" in *Companion to Classical Reception in Eastern and Central Europe,* eds. Zara Torlone, Dana Munteanu, and Dorota Deutsch (Chichester: Wiley-Blackwell, 2017), 300–311.

tru which it is; where the opposed senses of the individual and of the law merge and where the sliding toward something unknown but certain, as a becoming together, begins. What surprised in Brâncuşi's art was only that which should at all times define man's and the artist's works, a certain Against-Nature. Nature's works are of a kind: to place everything in transformation. Man's works are of a different kind, to settle everything, which means to place them in a different, better transformation.

In Brâncuşi, Against-Nature is truly human and good, in the way in which he organizes and depicts things. When he understands that the tendency of any thing that caught an embodiment is and must be detachment from gravity, non-dependence, entrance into a form of freedom, then he dreams flying throughout his life, and he makes it so that even a turtle flies, which means it is *întru* flying. This is because the appropriate placement of things takes place on a path. The entrance into order, as on an orbit, must be as the Romanian *aşterne-te drumului.*[7] It is probable that Brâncuşi would have liked the notion of Tao — as much as we can understand of it — just as he liked the Tibetan poet Milarepa. What he searches and finds is a path and a reason, a sense, a right guidance and placement in the bed of their flowing for everything that he was given to take in his Ark. Just as in Tao, there is no place for end in his view.

Indeed, what could be surprising as well in the artist Brâncuşi is that almost no work is finished, nor rounded, nor does it become unique; absolutely all of them could be resumed. In fact, the majority of them have been resumed by him, and they take on meaning only when you discern the artist's deeper thought, *întru* being. It is the thought of Tao, or the thought of Bach, and the thought of anyone who knows of order. Of course, you cannot finish once you enter into order. Despite of his admirable endings, Bach doesn't finish. For Brâncusi, too, you have no rest. The real in general doesn't rest by its immersion into order, by its

7 The expression combines two words that seem to have opposite meanings. *A se aşterne* means "to dwell," "to lay." When you lay yourself on the road, you start walking, you place yourself in the position of walking.

entrance into law and form. Such an inability to finish, in a positive sense, is also our preposition *întru,* and it even expresses its nature to be Path.

We will see one more time, at the end, what, truly speaking, this placement in being of Brâncuși is, and the extent to which it will lead to a good replacing and becoming, as well as the way in which becoming could be expressed precisely in the brute being of the stone and marble. We are now indebted to see if, for the unsuspected but significant joy of his creation, we cannot find antecedents in Romanian culture or language. We have already named the antecedent — the principal antecedent because it belongs to language and so to the matter in which everything that is creation is inscribed. It is the preposition *întru,* with its irradiation in everything that is Romanian.

We have invoked it at all times, in the description of the first face of being, according to our Romanian version, its darker face. We can now invoke the situation that *întru* brings for its bright face, under the sign of which was born, as a novelty in our world, Brâncuși's work, with its joy. Because we no longer deal with the tiresome elevation from common realities to a form of being but rather with being itself, this time we must study *întru* and *to be întru* in themselves. The Romanian sentiment of being must behold the state of being as well, not only the entrance in it. As far as common realities are concerned, it is expressed *by întru* or *due to întru,* as we showed, but it could also be expressed *as întru,* and thus as that entrance in order and discovery of the path that produces the serenity of Brâncuși's and a few others' work. We call it becoming *întru* being, and all the considerations *about întru* and *to be întru* will lead to it.

To Be *Întru*

Among prepositions, and all seem to have to do with sight, *întru* is a form of touch, having the full titles of this sense which is both common and special. All prepositions have indeed a spatial representation, as it has been observed: *in, to,* and *at,* in a sense also *with* and *without,* and clearly *under* and *above,* together with prepositional locutions, indicate something like a departure from a verb toward some noun. Only *întru* is not spatial; it indicates a different, more supple relation, which can comprise all prepositional relations as particular moments. Even more, it suggests a structure in which spatiality itself enters, as an opening in which unfolding in time can fit. In a word, it suggests a kind of field, spatial and temporal, static but moving, having a summary but an enlargement of this summary.

With *întru,* something goes deep into something else, enters in direct contact as in touch, grows together with it unmediated, co-grows and, far from being a simple composition, gives a fusion—just as it seemed that some Romanian words also give fusion, being representative for bundled, at times even opposed, meanings. It is significant that *întru* is often used with verbs or verbal nouns of transformation (*întru* falling asleep, discovery, fulfillment). Thus, it expresses becoming. In any case, it expresses proximity, intimacy, just as, at the limit, becoming *întru* being would express intimacy between becoming and being. All the other prepositions have something rigid in them and an aspiration toward exactness. Their precision, though, could appear only as a fixed moment in the indetermination of *întru*. Truly speaking, "in" is a simple moment of *întru,* as also "toward" (*înspre*); "with" is one of its aspects, just as "without." All prepositions, perhaps, in their rigidity, are particular cases of the processuality of *întru,* just as sight, hearing, smell, and taste were, for Aristotle as he said, forms of touch. First, it is the situation described by *întru,* then all the other prepositions with their situations come.

From all the prepositions that are inscribed in its matrix or are related with it, *întru* is detached mostly from in or inside, which gave it the semantic content while it was still *intro* in Latin. The latter has remained its poor relative compared to the richness of *întru*. It is the brother that delayed in a single sense and meaning. The extraordinary semantic evolution of *întru* in our language can best be emphasized by confronting *întru* with *înăuntru* ("inside"), and especially *to be întru* with "to be in."

With this example, you understand what the inventiveness and the genius of languages mean.

Compared to its original meaning of "to be in," the Romanian "to be *întru*" has begun to fly, just like Brâncuşi's statues. "To be in" remained to express the situation of closure, in all the meanings of closure. There are also good meanings of the closure of "to be in": shelter, rest, fixation, certainty, investment through something else, the happiness of belonging to a whole, the maternal bosom, and reintegration. Any creature, in a way, is "in" and seems to tend to be better in its great whole. But "to be in" represents at the same time rest and lethargy (that is, forgetfulness of action), renunciation and inertia. "To be *întru*" is detached from losing the self and forgetfulness, just as *întru* has detached from *intro,* gaining its autonomy. At the beginning, it can be a form of closure, and it even must be so, but it is a closure that knows to open itself. It is like waking up from sleep and moving to watchfulness. How can be the sleep of our matter, of our vegetative matter — sleep and dumbness, so the lack of utterance from the animal world — or the sleep, if not somnambulism, in which conscience itself can fall: how can they be better than the watchfulness of being that is completely open?

At a human level, though, the majority of beings still live *in* something, while their life would just begin if they came out of it. Man's education would represent, after all, the passing from a preposition into another, just this. People have too often been *under* something (under other people, under a devastating thought), or they were *with* something, as a simple phenomenon of accompanying, or *through* something, at times *without* something (perhaps especially without something, lamenting like Madame Bovary), other times coming *from* something and *out of* something; and they remained only this. Most often, they have been in something. They should have all been taken out from the regime of their prepositions and moved in the regime of *întru*. Life begins with to be *întru,* just as, for our world today, life is open *întru* future.

Even if they come alive for a moment, things and man are not necessarily steadfastly in the order of the living, but they can fall again among those that are inert when they fall from the condition of *to be întru,* so from the preposition of fulfillment back into stagnation. Every time, the entire problem of man is to come out of the inertia of prepositional situations in general and, in particular, from the situation of *to be in,* entering in a form of *to be întru*. Or, at the limit, it is to be in that form of to be *întru* that would no longer bring him back in *to be in.*

In their purity and as free structures, considered beyond man, *to be întru* and *to be in* have an entire bouquet of distinctive features.

To be in explains things without rest: this is how they are, in a whole in which every thing must be in its place. On the contrary, *to be întru* gives account of things by creating a rest. In the first situations, realities are the way they are, and they don't send to anything beyond themselves. In a way, they are numbered: everything is in order, without any deviation, and so without the possibility that the new would be born. *To be întru* gives or brings a rest to these realities, and only in this way, sending beyond themselves, can things be understood as bringing something in the world.

If it is this way, then a second distinctive feature could be that *to be întru* is not only at the end of things, with the superior placements of a human being, but also at their beginning, at the time when they take on being. With *to be in,* chaos is at peace. Things can be conceived as caught in the disorder of chaos and they have no way to come out of it. At each beginning of things, just as at the beginning of thought and of human situations with their chaos, *întru* works. It further remains in work and is that much more active as you rise further up on the stair of realities. Its virtues, though, can be seen from the beginnings, when it works alone.

Let us imagine a chaos, both in large scale, for the entire nature, and in small scale, for a creation that was not yet born (for man, for a decision or an act that have not yet been delineated). In chaos, of course, everything is in a state of untying. In other words, in its midst no preposition operates: nothing is on, in, under, with, or without. If now, in this total untying, a closure or rather a wrapping (as in the Cartesian theory of vortexes, for example) a situation is created in which the exercise of a first preposition, and only of it initially, becomes possible, that is, *întru*. Something, for example, enters in vibration and reverberates as a wave. But it does it *întru* that vibration from the beginning. In the world of the mind, something can be caught into a question, and the search that follows will be *întru* the horizon of that question or theme. Or, in the world of nature, as in the world of the mind, things can be caught in a symmetry, a polarity, or a form of antagonism. There is yet no fashion of *to be in* with them, but *to be întru* operates everywhere.

With a third distinctive feature, then, *to be in* expresses a well determined situation, a closure certain of itself, and after all, *exactness,* while *to be întru,* with its openness, tends to express something more than precision; let us say, something of the order of truth. *To be in,* so in good order and fixation, is the condition of the scientific. The exact scientific thinking endeavored to see how things in a field are *in* the law, *in* the whole, and exemplary scientific thinking, the one in mathematics, gave the paradigm of *to be in* with set theory. According to this fundamental theory, an element is in a set, belongs to a set, and a subset is also included in a set, and it only raises to its power as a paradox, in the infinite sets. The element or the subset cannot have the privilege of the point that Eminescu invoked and which could be master over the margins of the world.[8] They stay dutiful in their set, just as particular phenomena from various sciences stay dutiful under their law.

In this way, all of the sciences that we call "exact" and from which some strived to make the scientific model in general are

8 Noica refers to Mihai Eminescu's poem, "Letter I," which he has previously cited. "Suddenly, a point is moving… is the first, and one, and only. / Out of chaos, he makes mother, and the Father he becomes! / That point that is found in movement, weaker is than the seed of foam, / Is the master with no margins over the margins of the world."

under the sign of *to be in,* while the so-called human sciences,[9] which want more than exactness — they even want it even when they cannot obtain full exactness — search truth under the sign of *to be întru.* Perhaps, *to be in* and *to be întru* express better the difference between the two groups of sciences than it could have been done with the given names; our names would suggest something more primary. For there cannot be certain border between natural sciences or the sciences of exactness and human sciences. On the other hand, how can mathematics, which are sciences of "exactness," be other than human sciences first of all? It is about something more primary than sciences, methods, and fields. It is the opposition between *to be in* and *to be întru.* An irreducible conflict appears in this opposition, as it wasn't in the case of sciences and methods. If, with *to be întru,* you are not in the certainty and formal rigor in which *to be in* places you, you are, still, in a form of order that goes beyond *to be in.* It seems that it is the order that opens toward truth, as it will open toward being.

Perhaps a final difference between *to be in* and *to be întru* — if differences can be numbered and if they are not without end in their nuances — can best bring to light the opposition. In *to be in* the element as such is not interesting. It *is in* just as are all the others, having the same properties as they do. It doesn't represent something individual as such but a simple particular case, as every element is considered in sciences. On the contrary, with *to be întru,* the individual appears, different than the particular and together with it the promise of being, as it suggested it, with the three ontological terms, its possible model suggested above. The element is the one that is of interest now, in the situation brought by *to be întru,* because it is susceptible to rise to the power of the whole. Eminescu said about this point that is as a "seed of foam," that it was more valuable than the rest of the world. It could speak in the name of the entire world, as master of it. It could master and define it, as only one human specimen could rise from his individual to the human general, even

9 Noica includes here the humanities and social sciences.

at a bodily level, with the artistry of a runner or gymnast who expresses the dream of flying, of grace, of emancipation of our being, and this takes place much more at a spiritual level, where a single specimen can give the measure of the whole humanity. He is *întru* humanity, not *in* humanity.

This is how those of the spirit are *întru* values, and not *in* them. Nothing exists in, under, over, with (in which there wouldn't be any without) the value of beauty, for example; but *întru* it, things and beings can be. Indeed, what can there be *in* the fixity and rest of values? They can be only *întru* them. This is how it begins to be in the "exact" sciences, where some views, as the theory of systems, gain such importance today precisely because — we will dare say it — they know to bring into play the situation of *to be întru,* beyond the *to be in* which defined them exclusively in the past. Even the new science of cybernetics, which has so many practical applications, uses wittingly, and almost in a spirit of mechanic exactness, the situations of *to be întru,* with its homeostasis and inverse action, which makes the individual of a certain cybernetic system regain meaning in a world that had entered in the monotony of particular cases. The world of things now gains identity only by *to be întru.*

All of these could be read in the features that distinguished *to be in* and *to be întru.* Due to the analyzers that it brought into play, in the thought experience (how else could you call it?) of the Romanian language, *to be întru* has detached from *to be in* as much as the preposition *întru* has evolved compared to the other prepositions. Just like them, *întru* expresses a situation. It is not a principle of reality from which its phenomena could issue, nor a formal truth. (Even if one could conceive an organized view that would begin with today's formal systems, let us suppose that there is a vocable *întru* with a situation described by *to be întru.* What follows from here?) It is a mere situation. However, the situations that the other prepositions create are sketchy and frozen. The risk and the sterility of usual prepositions is precisely the expression of positions and placements that contain no tension. Even prepositions such as "toward" have within them the rest of a placement on a too certain direction. Our language liked to imagine by *întru* a preposition without an exact position, as a moving placement, or, in any case, charged by a tension. How little seems to have remain in *to be întru* from *to be in*!

However, with a remarkable control of thought and of the processualism that it brought, language made it so that *întru* maintained in it the memory of *in* and *inside,* from the Latin *intro*. Everywhere, we see things from the outside and any inside is seen from the outside. Here, with *întru,* the inside is seen from inside, as in a nuclear perspective. Man's subjectivity itself, so guilty before the exigence of the objectivity of exact sciences, becomes, at least once, a scientific privilege. Just as you understand what life is because you have life and as you understand what a human is because you are human, you can also understand what *to be întru* means because you are an intimity projected into the world. As your individual, you have the experience of individual reality placed *întru* something. And if the individual that is open toward a general is the first step toward being, with your self you can attempt to see what being is in itself.

On Being and the Two Becomings

You are *întru* something (a thought, a project, a meaning of life, a law). This means, in a sense, that you are surrounded and totalized by something that is stronger than you. Regardless of whether you chose to be *întru* it or you became conscious of having been *întru* it from the beginning, you understand the identity that this *shrouder,* which does not yet have an identity, gives to you. Thus, since you can no longer invest yourself without its nature, you search for its name, its definition, its boundaries. But nothing from the outside can show you its boundaries because you are and remain *întru* it. Everything you see is that the fact of being *întru* it constantly moves its boundaries from the inside so that the surrounder that gives you identity doesn't have a stable identity either, but it gains it together with yours.

Then, what confirms you needs your confirmation of it and depends on the measure of your power to confirm. Even if you cannot give it its full measure, you are not less of a carrier of its being, and the acknowledgement you offer it is the knowledge of its measure. The being *întru* which you are is, thus, at the level of your power of *înfiinţare* ("establishing").

Still, you are *întru* the being of the shrouder, and you're not a something-that-is[10] due to yourself. You are permanently beyond yourself, in the sense that you attempt to identify that which appears before you as a purpose, but that which is just as well your means to enter into your order. It is the horizon in which you are placed and in which, in fact, you re-place yourself at all times, just as in those answers that themselves bring questions to life. But at the same time, it is also your core, your organizing principle, just as totality is said in parts and is placed into meaning,[11] making them enter their meaning as well. Truer than its being and your being is your common being, your solidarity.

Solidarity is, on its turn, *întru* something, that is, *întru* this common fulfillment. When any exteriority is lost, then only the situation begins to have a name. It is that of *to be întru*.

This direct experience in human subjectivity, or better in a human's self, can describe something from the works that take place in any unfolded totality. In its open placement, *to be întru* was directed to a whole from the beginning, in whose bosom the part is and works. Contrary to other situations, where everything is also involved but is presupposed to preexist, *întru* is the one that makes it possible. *To be in* also implies a whole, but

---

10 We used "something-that-is" to translate the Romanian word *fiinţător,* "a thing that is." Noica suggests that you don't get your being from yourself but rather from the being of the so-called surrounder (that which surrounds you but not in the sense of things that are not you but rather as something that gives your being).

11 "Meaning" translates the Romanian term, *rost,* which we rendered as "sense" at the beginning of the paragraph. Rost encapsulates both these English terms, suggesting at the same time something that is given to you, a direction, and a revelation of the meaning of that direction.

every time a whole that is already given. *To be întru* can be in a whole that doesn't exist yet or, as the truths of today's science, gets educated as well.

With a part that is not truly a part and a whole that is not really stable, the universe of *to be întru* is now constituted. In this processualism, nothing maintains its identity, neither the whole nor the part, nor the horizon, the placement, the founding. All have been welded. All of them are of one, in *to be întru*. But all of them are also toward one. Totality in expansion, through the opening that was created in the field, is solved in one of concentration. *To be întru* expresses a first moment, the enlargement; now, totality has matured, being able to express restriction. That which is transformed, with *to be întru*, is only *întru* something, gathering the squandering of the world in its embodiments. But if you don't want to find certain embodiments, you can try to see here the pure exercise of open structure, from the totality in expansion to the part that carries the whole, to the totality closed as a horizon above the part; then to the totality that is welded with the part, the one that became principle of organization and orientation of the part, to the totality of restriction and focalization into a point.

This is how being itself is: a whole which is not a given whole, even if it could be said that the being of the world is the totality in expansion of those that are in the world. It is rather a whole that goes toward every part, making so that each part is a bearer of being, of a whole. It is a totality that surrounds the part, as one of its horizons. It merges with the part, becoming its intimacy and its principle of organization and determining everything that is to tend toward a being in the bosom of which it is from the beginning, to search for that which it already possesses, to orient itself toward its own meaning, and to go deep in it as in a unique foundation.

This is how truth is also; a totality that cannot remain in the simple totality of truths in the plural but that is so that any partial truth should rise to the power of truth. Or there is a horizon around any approach to truth. But isn't there, at the same time, everything that is more intimate in each truth? In the situation created by *to be întru,* the paradox of truth, signaled by the ancients and that you cannot recognize it unless you already know it, begins to lose its sharpness. Just like being, truth is not followed because it is totally unknown, but a certain knowledge of it is the one that opens the field for its search. This is because that knowledge is first the science of organization and of the orientation of a search with the desire to find truth in concentration and not in expansion, as at the beginning, still according to the model of *to be întru.*

Întru is, thus, a happy vocable of resettlement, of becoming. Everything that *is* is something else, culture says after all. The immediate is not immediate, but it is itself distant, just as science sees the law in the individual, or art the essential in the real. But the greatest resettlement is the one that thinking itself gives. According to the ancients, the theme of thinking was being. According to some moderns, its theme was becoming. What if the real theme, from beyond all of these, was the becoming of truth itself and the becoming *întru* being?

If we assumed, for a moment, that becoming opposes being — as it has too often been said, with the risk of transforming becoming into a dissolution and being into a frost — then it should also be acknowledged that the Romanian language and spirit have especially the organ of being. The modality of duration, of permanence (duration and permanence being presupposed attributes of being) has produced uncommonly many adverbs in our language, and an adverb is the one that creates the more subtle balance of thought for it places its worries, the verbs, in order. We say: always, eternally, ever, forever, steadfastly, or all the time, and this is beyond the common formations as in other languages, with negative prefixes: never-endingly, unceasingly, unbreakingly, or unendingly. But if we have direct reference to "being" by so many expressions, we also have an instrument of investigation for becoming, perhaps an irreplaceable one, *întru,* which will bring us back to being, together with becoming this time.

Becoming can only be *întru* something, respectively *întru* something that holds. It presupposes a form of consistency. That which is in a process of untying doesn't have becoming but only movement, change, semblance, or succession, development, unfolding, evolution, or transformation. None of those can be substituted to becoming, even if becoming presupposes all of them.

A river doesn't become; it flows. A mathematical transformation doesn't become; it unfolds. The various states of weather do not become, but they succeed each other. None of these manifestations of reality have place by necessity *întru* something. Becoming appears, in them and with them from simple movement to transformation, only the moment when an embodiment of the situation described by *to be întru* has been obtained by nature or man. What is *întru* something becomes; and it becomes the very thing (the horizon, the whole) *întru* which it is something; or, welded together, they become the part and the whole, a thing and its horizon, the surrounded with its shrouder. Only a totality of every moment is able to become, so something that, by becoming, reestablishes itself steadfastly as totality.

It is known that the ancients had no understanding for becoming. According to them, when something is indeterminate, it is in nonbeing in the only form of nonbeing for them, that is, indistinct matter. When something is in actuality, it means that it is fulfilled, being in its achieved purpose. Thus, there would be no place for becoming between nonbeing and being but only for the violent act of birth. Something would be either in the target[12] or outside of its target.

But isn't here a third modality, being *întru* target? This is what becoming is, which doesn't express the ends of a path but the path itself, including its ends. That which is in becoming has departed from the non-form of prime matter, but it is not in the fully obtained form of the reached end. It is *întru* that form, together with it, being modeled by it and making so that it itself is modeled by becoming. This is why the ancients do not have the problem of becoming even if they implied it always; or, if

12 Noica uses the term "target" with the meaning of telos.

they have one, it is the extreme problem of Heraclitus, with its risk of dissolution.

If you confront *to be întru* with the view of some of the moderns, you find yourself in the opposite situation, that of becoming without ends. This is, at least, how Nietzsche understood it, when he said in the 357th aphorism from *Die fröhliche Wissenschaft,*[13] "We, the Germans, are Hegelians even if Hegel didn't exist, in the measure in which [...] he attributed the instinct of becoming and unfolding a fuller meaning and value than to 'that which is'; we hardly give credence to the justification of a notion as such as that of being."

In this interpretation, it is possible that we rather have the Nietzschean and Goethean theme of a becoming "beyond good and evil" than about Hegel's view. But it is not less true that being and nonbeing could have seemed anterior to becoming, at least logically, since becoming represented their synthesis. *To be întru,* on the contrary, expresses such an original situation for becoming that it may be said, from its perspective, that being and nonbeing do not make becoming, but they unfold from it. Just as in modern physics certain particles get decomposed in elements out of which they have never been composed, the lesson of *to be întru* is that being and nonbeing are terms toward which becoming opens, into which it is unfolded. With this, real world, with its good and evil, with its fulfillment or disaggregation, comes out of the blind innocence of becoming, so out of neutrality.

For *întru* what do things become? Either *întru* that which is, or, appearing for just a moment, *întru* that which is not. Being and nonbeing considered in isolation are seconds. The one who is in the horizon of being and nonbeing cannot ask oneself of a being and nonbeing of first instance. However, what is in their horizon can enlarge their horizon, even if it cannot come out of

13 Friedrich Nietzsche, *Die fröhliche Wissenschaft* [*The Gay Science*] (1882). Noica doesn't mention the edition he uses. We translated the text from Romanian.

it. That which becomes can increase and decrease the beings of the world.

Being appears as a novelty. It is the same situation in man's case, which is more expressive than the case of things in making becoming and its chances of being evident. Normally, man is in something, staying under one or other totality of nature and of society, where, as individual, he has neither being nor nonbeing. Man is thus numbered, so he is a specimen among specimen, as in an extinct theory of sets. Closed in this manner, he finds himself already surrendered to statistics. Various things can happen to him, so that he has movement, change, renewal, transformation, and even evolution, but he cannot enter in becoming by himself. Where does becoming begin, either the historical one, of collectivities, or the individual one? Where do the chances of coming out of statistics begin for man and society?

In the case of an individual, it is simple. When he enters under the attraction of a truth, of a meaning in life, or of a modeling idea, he conquers the condition of *to be in* and goes into that of *to be întru* something. This term of attraction may not be a truth, a meaning, or an idea already constituted. They may even never be constituted for the one who opens toward them and becomes at the same time with them. Nevertheless, it is not less the term *întru* which becoming takes place, the term to which becoming relates steadfastly, even if it embodies it differently every time. Human knowledge thus enters in becoming—under a truth that is both found and searched for, just as the life of a human individual (specimen), taken out of statistics, or of a collectivity that has been integrated in the historical process—and enters in the becoming under a meaning or just as their commonly human productivity passes into creativity *întru* a form of superior and consciously registered harmony. Only then novelty is born, with the chances of bringing about being, which is always something unexpected to the world.

Becoming, though, starts from below, from under man, from things, even from those inanimate. For, just as that which is alive may not have becoming, that which is inanimate may enter into its schemes, which seemed to be the privilege of life. Even chaotic matter is worth of such a privilege, thus bringing becoming and novelty in its own world.

In the known universe, novelty and the preparation of being by becoming are first brought by a wave in physics. A wave is a way of *to be întru* the initial vibration, which is resumed and which leads to becoming in its elementary purity, identical becoming.

However, the simple becoming of a wave is fixed in the becoming of dead matter, which is always a package of waves. A different way of *to be întru* will know to find again becoming in the bosom or with the elements of that which becomes. It is the organic, which comes out from the prison of *to be in*. We know today that the organic is instituted by a genetic code and that its sense of existence is a *to be întru* that code. Now, becoming is no longer spectral, as in the case of a wave, but real, and it is no longer one of identity but one of diversification within the biotype or bio-model.

How clear it appears, in the case of the organic, that any becoming is a concrete modality of the situation described by *to be întru*. A new perspective of the emergence of being is born with the restoration of becoming in the organic. Until now, being was only a vibration with the wave, or an ensemble of elements with the inorganic becoming: things pretended to be, but they were not truly. At the most, they had an infused being, that form of consistency that any becoming brings into play in its unfolding or its unfolded. With the organic, though, becoming is installed in the bosom of reality and brings an extraordinary novelty to our land, which was not known either by the wave or the inorganic, that is, the increasing being.

How could you believe that being is a way of freezing of things, or the things' fixed image in elements? Growth and increase, fulfillment and differentiation can only belong to being; and the notions that are not looking for being into such growing becoming, but rather in eternal elements of ultimate meanings, end up either in nuclear particles or in the ineffable, as in Heidegger.

The organic has assumed something from the expansion of the wave, which is distributed without being divided as life is distributed without being divided. It has overflowed over the world of the becoming of this step, which is fixed inorganic matter, from the most modest seminal beginnings, having a power of spreading that you must name as belonging to being, having otherwise the risk of no longer saying something meaningful about being. The organic overcomes the massiveness of the inorganic wherever it appears precisely due to the strength of becoming that is bearer of being over the one that has become and has blocked being.

However, the amount of being that the organic can express is shown by itself. If it opens toward being, it doesn't institute it truly because its becoming is closed over being itself. This becoming diversifies the type *întru* which it is, but it cannot come out of its condition, and it unceasingly resumes. In the case of the organic, *to be întru* is only *întru* what is given to it. Only man will be able to become *întru* something else than he previously is. Only he will give the premises of being. The nature of the organic comes up only to a fulfillment that is resumed, as the specimen remake themselves within the species and become to the level where they can bring onto the world a new existence, which would become itself as well. The condition of the organic is the unceasing repetition, and its becoming ends by being *întru* further becoming.

There are two becomings that are gathered together in man but with different orientations: one a becoming *întru* becoming and the other *întru* being. The first has been understood as becoming itself, opposed to the idea of being, as in Nietzsche's quote and Goethe's view. However, it must also be understood in terms of being, as its unfulfillment. On the contrary, becoming *întru* being can be recognized as the thesis of being.

Those that thought and invoked being overwhelmed man too much with its massiveness. We must be emancipated, not overcome by it. Being is a *lysis,* a releasing, and not something given, behind us or before us. Or, if it is both behind us and before us, it is as a "you wouldn't have looked for me if you hadn't already found me," a great, interminable novelty.

Since *întru* is what gave us the suggestion of the becoming *întru* being, Romanian infuse thinking about being must have a special character. Indeed, a different sentiment of being than that of heaviness has come to the surface in any Romanian view. Being has a good, positive freedom here. The world is not under being nor in being; rather, it is *întru* it. Thus, the world has the freedom to remain in becoming, which means in searching and finding and at times even in wandering, with or without the memory of being.

For we can speak of two becomings. One is that which is turned on itself, a becoming only *întru* something, as a ceaseless repetition, satisfied or unsatisfied of itself, being able to represent a real forgetfulness of being. The other is the becoming with the aspiration of being in it. The world of man is divided according to these two becomings, just as his world and culture in its entirety are as well.

Man lives, acts, and creates under this double becoming. There is no way for becoming *întru* being to be triumphant by itself in human existence. The part of becoming *întru* becoming is still overwhelming in man. The biorhythms of nature place their seal over everything that is vegetability and animality in human being, and man lives under the continual remaking of life, as in a becoming *întru* becoming that he may idealize at times but which he cannot evade. At the same time, in the superior zones of his existence, as society or individual, man can live under various forms of becoming *întru* becoming.

Becoming *întru* becoming has so much refined within the framework of human existence that an entire domain of man's free creation, a creation that seemed to be of the order of a tentative of a becoming *întru* being, risks to remain in the limits of a becoming *întru* becoming if man doesn't find his place in the world and in society. It is about technology. In itself, technology is a novelty in the bosom of nature with a different style and horizon. By its success and proliferation, technology entered in a becoming like the one of nature, within Western society, increasing, often blindingly, and bringing on the world various creatures with or without necessity. Even more than that, it can lead to a potentiation of nature in man and outside of him, which would show the nonsense of his becoming *întru* becoming; at the limit, it can lead to an "ageless youth and deathless life," so to a prolongation of life that wouldn't have suitable content for man as it leads to so many means that don't serve a clear purpose but rather become purposes unto themselves, and then they are to be repudiated because they mystify the idea of human purpose.

There is a strange phenomenon in the second half of the twentieth century: the youth of societies that know only how to be consumer societies, on the basis of higher technology, this youth raised against a fulfillment as fulfillment of needs. This phenomenon could be understood as an exacerbation of the awareness that becoming *întru* becoming, now refined to the level of man, is sovereign in its world. An entire world of bourgeois civilization triumphs, but it is also shaken at its core, under the sign of becoming *întru* becoming.

However, what is striking for man is not the fact that becoming *întru* becoming has taken such refined forms that it leads to exasperation. Despite some appearances of exclusivity that lead to the sentiment of the nonsense of life and society, becoming *întru* becoming has always been intimately woven with the potentiality of becoming *întru* being. For man, everything beginning from biology and going up is duplication; everything is distributed according to becoming *întru* becoming, on the one hand, and becoming *întru* being, on the other.

How surprising and still clearly inscribed in man is the presence of the two forms of becoming, even in this product of society, language. If you understand that the entire work of languages can be concentrated in words, just as various works of thought are concentrated in concepts, then you can see a genuine becoming *întru* becoming in a word. Usually, with its purpose of communication, a word carries within it a simple becoming *întru* becoming, and the contents of thought become obligatory in the same way — as it happens in languages artificially constructed — and they refashion themselves rhythmically only *întru* it. But the word itself, with its horizon of meanings, is an open totality in the real life of languages. The becoming of thoughts *întru* it increases its being and charges it with ever more being. In a way, this pendulation between the two becomings takes place with every word, but, for some words, the amplitude of pendulation is significant for the strength of the thought.

One of the most beautiful illustrations for the becoming *întru* being of words is found in the Romanian word *cădere* ("fall"). With its vertiginous crash, this word seems to only express the meaning passed onto it by its Latin prototype. *A cădea* can only be *a cădea*; at the most, *a cădea bine,*[14] *a se potrivi,* as the Latin word could also suggest. But as with everything connected with man, a becoming took place with this word, and it began not only to fall more smoothly, but also to express the various cases, placements, and situations of things up to their casuistic and even to show how they unfold in an organized manner at the same time with their cadences. If the becoming of this word corrected its vertical fall into a horizontal unfolding in other neo-Latin languages as well, in our language, the becoming *întru* being of this word sent it further to the point of investing it truly with the titles of being. This is because the curve of semantic becoming of *a cădea* began, surprisingly, to climb. If the verb *a cădea, cădere,* still maintains the initial meaning, the verbal noun, *cădere,* with the same form, then can mean investment: to have *căderea* to be, to do something.

Being so, our word is, in a sense, the description of the very trajectory on which becoming is inscribed, what it means at its origin, with *de-venio* (as *de-duco,* or *de-currere, decursus*), a coming down from above, a becoming *întru* generation and corruption, so *întru* disappearance, as the ancients used to say;

---

14 *A cădea bine,* translated word by word with "to fall well," requires an indirect object. Something "falls well" to someone, as when something matches someone well, so *a se potrivi.* For example, after a meal that you really like and that also makes you feel good, you could say, *mi-a căzut bine,* "it fell well to me."

then, it passes to the moderns *întru* becoming; and, for both ancients and moderns, after all, it is the becoming that may have the *cădere,* so the dignity, the status to institute being. This word has the *cădere,* the status, to say what is to be done and what is not to be done (what *se cade* and what *nu se cade*), what holds and what doesn't hold, in other words what has *căderea* to be, the final *cădere,* respectively ascent.

If we have spoken of the becoming *întru* becoming of a word in general, semantically, we could just as well discuss a becoming *întru* being of a word in the ontological sense, so of a passing of the word into being. For the ancients, it was a problem if it was about something natural or conventional, in the case of the word. But today's science, which integrated the word among signs with semiotics, could show the ontological strength that the word, the code, and the sign have, since you call and maneuver things by the word, the code, and the sign. Today, cosmic objects are called on their names (by waves and code), and the creatures of the earth begin to appear the same way, with their genetic codes. But what does being mean if not that which makes things be together with their way and with the result of this way? In the history of man, the word has become *întru* being, literally.

There are then two becomings everywhere in the world of man. When becoming *întru* becoming—which is aroused by man and paralleled to the becoming *întru* becoming aroused by nature, both from outside and from within man's being—brings so much earthquake to the world with its *demonia* (modern, Western technology), we must remember the large and good part that becoming *întru* being has in man, even if it is not without risks. Together with it, man's approaches and conceptions enter in duplication. There will be, for example, a time of becoming *întru* becoming, which is perhaps time itself with its usual meaning; but a time of becoming *întru* being also appeared together with man, with his deeds, and with his becoming that creates meaning.

Will there be other couplings with the becoming *întru* being? Will there be another spatiality, another temporality? In any case, the new space and the new time of creation will appear. Let us illustrate this becoming *întru* being of the creator that was obtained in the Romanian view of the world with one of the strangest creators who appeared in the history of culture, Brâncuşi.

Becoming *întru* Being

We will try to illustrate being as being with a Romanian creation. Everything — Romanian presentiments, feelings, and notions that were detached from popular and educated creations of our history, not to mention the genius of the language — everything, then, led us to an answer regarding the being of things. But what about being as being, the one that emerges from the depth of *to be întru,* as becoming *întru* being? We dare to illustrate it with an aspect, perhaps the essential one, of Brâncuşi's creation, which is imbued with a barely beginning philosophical conscience, both popular and educated.

There's something striking in the work of this Romanian sculptor. Even if someone were to contest its value, no one could contest its character of universality, which is perhaps unique in the history of art. This is not the case for human spectators only, be them educated or not, who could be made to understand something from Brâncuşi's *Rooster,* for example, or from a bird's flight or from the *Infinity Column*; we include here extraterrestrial spectators. Any creation of art (such as the Parthenon, the cathedrals, the *Venus of Milo,* and Rodin's *Thinker,* even a monument which is not meant to be art but carries the spirit within it, such as the Pyramids) would not be intelligible in itself to an extraterrestrial being. It would be necessary to give him minimal explanations. On the contrary, at least a few of Brâncuşi's works can be directly understood.

When Brâncuşi's *Rooster* — or one of his roosters, since almost all of his works have isotopes, as in the Romanian view of being, and as the substances of the world have — was placed in front of the Parthenon some years ago, Brâncusi's artistry received, without a doubt, a tribute. But hasn't the intelligibility of his art received a tribute by that as well? Even more, we will claim that, independently of the intrinsic artistic value of ancient work of art compared to the work of our contemporary artist, a great stranger would understand something from the *Rooster,* while he would raise his elbows (if he had elbows) before the Parthenon, being that much more perplexed as the Parthenon would be restored to its original form.

One may say this: on the one hand, we have a work of art with a spiritual content; on the other, a sort of scheme and a suggestion of work of art. But isn't a pyramid a scheme as well? And don't Brâncuşi's works also have a spiritual content?

All human creations seem to have an "inside = *inside,*" as the pyramid has its hidden tomb. On the contrary, something of the *Rooster*'s order has an "inside = *outside.*" It has the revealed essence of the thing, that is, a song that grows, a creature or a throat that grow; in a word, a growing, like in the case of the column, and such a thing is perceived by anyone, even if that person has no idea about a rooster and its cock-a-doodle-doo.

Brâncuşi's works are in the universal of being, in "essence," as he himself says. They are no longer in simple existence. This means that they are truly in the universal of being, expressing something from being as being. Even a work that expresses rather a particular being, as *Mademoiselle Pogany*—and that much more a specific creature, but in its generality, as *Sleeping Muse, Măiastra, Flying Turtle*—enter in the general being, when it is resumed in other versions. If the foreigner didn't understand what a face of Mademoiselle Pogany represents, he would understand the isotopes of the same creature and would see in them what we suggest for being itself, that is, a kind of becoming *întru* being of a creature, which reflects becoming *întru* being in general. If, similarly, he didn't get the flight from the flight of one bird, he would understand the universality and a form of essential being in the resumed flights.

How could he not see something with meaning in *The Table of Silence* or *The Infinity Column*? In the case of the *Table,* it may be clear to him that there is not only a presence, in central object with its cubs, its multiple, or its organization; but it would also be clear that there is an absence as well, that the *Table* with the chairs around it are waiting for something or are left by something, like the atom that is ionized by losing an electron. Everything he knows (and the extraterrestrial stranger must know something: *counting,* so unity and multiplicity, *birth* of living things, so prefiguration and life, *rational thought,* so openness of a plethora of thoughts from one thought) can be inscribed not in the scheme, but in the concrete of this *Table of Silence,* which is, after all, also of speech, as it is a Table of Death and also of Life.

As for the *Column,* whoever does not know anything about the Romanian becoming *întru* being, so about the answer that we could suggest — of course, only suggest — to Aristotle's centuries-long question (What is "being as being?") should watch the *Infinity Column* attentively. If he wants the mechanical, he has the most splendid mechanical unfolding. If he wants the organic, he fully sees the growth node by node, the vertebration and the organic itself. If, finally, he wants the image of the spirit, he finds the most perfect chain reaction of thought there. Does he want the infinite? But this is precisely what is offered to him there, encapsulated. All of these things are possible because Brâncuși began to sculpt being as being.

However, he actually considered that it was "becoming *întru* being," as Romanian thought senses it as well. His creation proves to be that much more significant for thought as it is about sculpture, so the art of statuary being, on the one hand, and about stone, so the matter of inert being, on the other hand.

Indeed, sculpture is the art of being by excellence, of the Apollonian, to which Dionysian becoming is opposed. Parmenides, with his unmoved being, was the philosophical genius of the Apollonian, providing the image of the absolute Sculpture, the sphere. However, for a peasant's son from Hobița,[15] sculpture is no longer the art of being but of a strange becoming, which we identify as becoming *întru* being. According to the Romanian

15 The southwestern Romanian town where Brâncuși was born.

sentiment of being, just as becoming *întru* being wobbles, the artist makes stillness wobble.

Thought also felt the need to weave becoming with being. In a sense, the problem of a reconciliation between Parmenides, the priest of being, and Heraclitus, the prophet of becoming, was raised since Plato, but the reconciliation was difficult with renunciations and concession on both sides. In our days, purely speculative thinking attempted something even more risky than Platonism; Heidegger endeavored to show that Heraclitus and Parmenides do not need to be reconciliated because they are indeed one, even if the historians of thought, beginning with Plato, acknowledged a genuine opposition between the two. Thus, today's thinker must himself bring violence to these sayings in order to be able to marry one's becoming with the other's being. Becoming *întru* being comes to say simply that Heraclitus, considered at least symbolically, *is* truly one with Parmenides and is also considered symbolically one, even if historically they were opposed. Brâncuși doesn't say it, but he places it before our eyes through sculpture.

Brâncuși expresses through sculpture its contrary, fluidity. He even goes further, to the generality of matter (stone, marble, bronze, anything) and even to its essence, in order to propose its contrary to it. Anything matter would be, unless it is a flake or a dandelion down, it can only express heaviness, while Brâncuşi wants it to express lightness, flight, just as the Romanian sentiment intuited the freedom of being instead of its gravity.

The two great ontological orders, being and becoming, were merged, reminding of the way in which Romanian language merges opposite meanings by welding them, not composing them exteriorly. From here, we can see the simplicity with which Brâncuși can make the impossible to take a familiar face and a world of fairytales to become reality. In fact, the artist doesn't impose a fairy world to natural reality. He actually finds it in the bosom of reality, just as Romanian folklore finds the enchanting world of fairytales everywhere. In the city where Brâncuşi raised his *Infinity Column*, one can still see stone boulders in the garden of the house where he used to stay, smoothed not by the artist but by waters. Brâncuşi had found in the water of Jiu[16] a direct expression for a kind of becoming *întru* being of the stone.

In the same way as when he sees the impossible or he obtains it simply in nature, he gives it a face of reality, in the flights expressed through stone or a different material and in the plurality of a person or of a unique creature, rendered in a different way than how Rembrandt was doing in time, successively, his self-portraits. We are no longer in the time of flow; but we are in a kind of time and in a form of flow. As a new conquered impossibility, sculpted simply, he reduces the infinite to the scale of man and captures the uncapturable in sculpture.

The fact that he succeeded in rendering the infinite in finite, the flight in fixity and in inert matter, identity in a plurality that is not repetition; the fact that he could place under anyone's eyes the becoming in the order of being, showing that being *is* and must *be* only in this way, as becoming *întru* being, all of these he expressed in a simple statue from the beginning of his career, *Sophrosyne or Wisdom of the Earth,* a statue that represents perhaps his first thought as it could represent the first thought or something from the first day when the Earth started to think.

16 River in Romania, in the region where Brâncuşi was born.

APPENDIX I

The Evening Star / Luceafărul

Mihai Eminescu
trans. *Octavian Gabor*[1]

1 I want to thank several people who have offered feedback on this translation. First of all, Eveline Băeşu, Dana LaCourse Munteanu, and Magdalena Sas. I also want to thank Stefan Cojocaru, Ioana and Horia Groza, Mark Klus, Fr. Ciprian Sas, and Fr. Timotei Sas. Most of all, my thanks go to Lily Brewer, from punctum books, who offered invaluable feedback. I encourage readers to read other translations of the same poem as well (I mentioned some of them in chapter 4, where Noica discusses "The Evening Star"), so that they get a more complete view of the poem. Its full beauty stems from a perfect combination of melody, word-choice, and philosophy. From my part, if this translation encourages people to read Eminescu in the original, I consider my mission accomplished.

A fost odată ca-n povești,
A fost ca niciodată,
Din rude mari împărătești,
O prea frumoasă fată.

Și era una la părinți
Și mândră-n toate cele,
Cum e Fecioara între sfinți
Și luna între stele.

Din umbra falnicelor bolți
Ea pasul și-l îndreaptă
Lângă fereastră, unde-n colț
Luceafărul așteaptă.

Privea în zare cum pe mări
Răsare și străluce,
Pe mișcătoarele cărări
Corăbii negre duce.

Îl vede azi, îl vede mâni,
Astfel dorința-i gata;
El iar, privind de săptămâni,
Îi cade dragă fata.

Cum ea pe coate-și răzima
Visând ale ei tâmple
De dorul lui și inima
Și sufletu-i se împle.

Și cât de viu s-aprinde el
În orișicare sară,
Spre umbra negrului castel
Când ea o să-i apară.

*

It was upon a time in truth,
As if it never happened,
From mighty parents came a youth,
A most beautiful maiden.

She was a single lamb, no taints,
Her beauty above all masters,
Just like the Virgin among saints,
The moon among the asters.

And from the shade of mighty vaults,
She steps toward the window
So with the star she has a waltz…
His expectation does grow.

She watched him far, how on the sea,
He rises, always shines forth,
On moving path, black boats are free,
He leads them pointing their north.

She sees him now, morrow again,
And thus desire is formed;
And, week by week, he also deigns
To watch her: to her he's warmed.

And on her elbows, as she dreams,
She places her sweet temples,
With longing for him her heart beams,
Her soul inside her trembles.

And how alive he takes more light
Night by night, without fears,
Toward the shadow of the site
Where she to him appears.

*

Și pas cu pas pe urma ei
Alunecă-n odaie,
Țesând cu recile-i scântei
O mreajă de văpaie.

Și când în pat se-ntinde drept
Copila să se culce,
I-atinge mâinile pe piept,
I-nchide geana dulce;

Și din oglindă luminiș
Pe trupu-i se revarsă,
Pe ochii mari, bătând închiși
Pe fața ei întoarsă.

Ea îl privea cu un surâs,
El tremura-n oglindă,
Căci o urma adânc în vis
De suflet să se prindă.

Iar ea vorbind cu el în somn,
Oftând din greu suspină
– „O, dulce-al nopții mele domn,
De ce nu vii tu? Vină!

Cobori în jos, luceafăr blând,
Alunecând pe-o rază,
Pătrunde-n casă și în gând
Și viața-mi luminează!"

El asculta tremurător,
Se aprindea mai tare
Și s-arunca fulgerător,
Se cufunda în mare;

And step by step, behind her trace,
He slides'n the lass's chamber,
His bitter cold sparks weave a lace
Of flames that seem of ember.

And when the maiden goes to bed
To sleep her night of roses,
Her hands he touches, on her spread,
And gently her eyes closes.

And from the mirror, indiscreet,
He overflows her figure,
Her wide eyes sealed, yet beat by beat,
Her face came to transfigure.

She smiled at him with a slight gleam,
He trembled in the mirror,
For he pursued her in a dream
And to her soul drew near.

And while she spoke with him in sleep,
A sigh is born in tear:
"Oh, sweetest lord of my night, leap!
Why don't you come? Appear!

Descend, oh, gentle evening star,
Upon a beam glide here,
My home and thought all yours they are,
Transform my life in cheer!"

He listened, trembling, passion-filled,
Brighter for the king's daughter,
And suddenly, as he was thrilled,
He sank into the water.

Și apa unde-au fost căzut
În cercuri se rotește,
Și din adânc necunoscut
Un mândru tânăr crește.

Ușor el trece ca pe prag
Pe marginea ferestei
Și ține-n mână un toiag
Încununat cu trestii.

Părea un tânăr voevod
Cu păr de aur moale,
Un vânăt giulgi se-ncheie nod
Pe umerele goale.

Iar umbra feței străvezii
E albă ca de ceară -
Un mort frumos cu ochii vii
Ce scânteie-n afară.

– „Din sfera mea venii cu greu
Ca să-ți urmez chemarea,
Iar cerul este tatăl meu
Și mumă-mea e marea.

Ca în cămara ta să vin,
Să te privesc de-aproape,
Am coborât cu-al meu senin
Și m-am născut din ape.

O, vin'! odorul meu nespus,
Și lumea ta o lasă;
Eu sunt luceafărul de sus,
Iar tu să-mi fii mireasă.

And where he fell, row after row,
The sea in circles surges,
And from the concealed depth below
A proud, young man emerges.

Over the window's edge he goes
As if a threshold passes,
And in his hands a rod he holds
With reeds that seem like tasses.

He seemed a young, tall voivode
With golden, tender hair;
A livid shroud fell on his broad
Shoulders that seemed so bare.

The shadow of his lucid face
Is white as made of beeswax,
A dead man with lit eyes from space
That sparkle into climax.

"From my own sphere I have come
With pain, thy voice to honor,
The darken sea below's my mum,
And heaven is my father.

To hold thy face onto my palm
I have come to thy quarters,
I have descended from my calm,
And I was born from waters.

Oh, come my one and only love,
Thy world behind leave, dear!
I am the evening star above,
Be thou my bride, sincere.

Colo-n palate de mărgean
Te-oi duce veacuri multe,
Și toată lumea-n ocean
De tine o s-asculte."

– „*O, ești frumos, cum numa-n vis*
Un înger se arată,
Dară pe calea ce-ai deschis
N-oi merge niciodată;

Străin la vorbă și la port,
Lucești fără de viață,
Căci eu sunt vie, tu ești mort,
Și ochiul tău mă-nghează."

*

Trecu o zi, trecură trei
Și iarăși, noaptea, vine
Luceafărul deasupra ei
Cu razele-i senine.

Ea trebui de el în somn
Aminte să-și aducă
Și dor de-al valurilor domn
De inim-o apucă

– „*Cobori în jos, luceafăr blând,*
Alunecând pe-o rază,
Pătrunde-n casă și în gând
Și viața-mi luminează!"

Cum el din cer o auzi,
Se stinse cu durere,
Iar ceru-ncepe a roti
În locul unde piere;

To high palaces come with me,
For centuries you'll glisten,
And all the creatures of the sea
To thou will bow and listen."

"Oh, beautiful you are… In dream
Such angels do appear,
But to this path that's so extreme
I will never get near.

A stranger both in word and deed,
You shine, a lifeless figure,
You're dead, and I'm alive, indeed,
Your cold eyes make me shiver."

*

A day has passed, and then two more,
The night, again, appears,
The evening star comes as before
With his rays clear like spears.

She had to bring him back to mind,
The lord of waves unshaken,
In sleep, she longing for his kind,
Her heart is overtaken.

"Descend, oh, gentle evening star,
Upon a beam now glide here,
My home and thought all yours they are,
Transform my life in sweet cheer!"

And when he hears again her cry,
His light in much pain dies out,
And on his place high in the sky
Circles in waves do turn out.

În aer rumene văpăi
Se-ntind pe lumea-ntreagă,
Și din a chaosului văi
Un mândru chip se-ncheagă;

Pe negre vițele-i de păr
Coroana-i arde pare,
Venea plutind în adevăr
Scăldat în foc de soare.

Din negru giulgi se desfășor
Marmoreele brațe,
El vine trist și gânditor
Și palid e la față;

Dar ochii mari și minunați
Lucesc adânc himeric,
Ca două patimi fără saț
Și pline de-ntuneric.

– *„Din sfera mea venii cu greu*
Ca să te-ascult ș-acuma,
Și soarele e tatăl meu,
Iar noaptea-mi este muma;

O, vin', odorul meu nespus,
Și lumea ta o lasă;
Eu sunt luceafărul de sus,
Iar tu să-mi fii mireasă.

O, vin', în părul tău bălai
S-anin cununi de stele,
Pe-a mele ceruri să răsai
Mai mândră decât ele."

The air is filled with fiery flames,
Over the whole world they spread,
And from the chaos without names
Is born a proud and young head.

And on his black flocks of his hair
His crown seems to take fire,
In truth he came flying through air,
Bathing in the sun's choir.

From his black shroud, quite ostensive,
His arms are white as marbles.
He comes in sadness, and pensive,
His paleness causes marvels.

But his enchanting and large eyes
Gleam deep; they are chimeric,
Just like two passions, no allies,
A darkness atmospheric.

"From my own sphere have I come
Again, thy voice to honor,
The dark and cold night is my mum,
And heaven is my father.

Oh, come my one and only love,
Thy world behind leave, my dear!
I am the evening star above,
Be thou my bride in my sphere.

Oh, come, and in your golden hair
The stars will be suspended,
And there's no one that is more fair,
More proud, and yes, more splendid"

– „O, ești frumos cum numa-n vis
Un demon se arată,
Dară pe calea ce-ai deschis
N-oi merge niciodată!

Mă dor de crudul tău amor
A pieptului meu coarde,
Și ochii mari și grei mă dor,
Privirea ta mă arde."

– „Dar cum ai vrea să mă cobor?
Au nu-nțelegi tu oare,
Cum că eu sunt nemuritor,
Și tu ești muritoare?"

– „Nu caut vorbe pe ales,
Nici știu cum aș începe -
Deși vorbești pe înțeles,
Eu nu te pot pricepe;

Dar dacă vrei cu crezământ
Să te-ndrăgesc pe tine,
Tu te coboară pe pământ,
Fii muritor ca mine."

– „Tu-mi ceri chiar nemurirea mea
În schimb pe-o sărutare,
Dar voi să știi asemenea
Cât te iubesc de tare;

Da, mă voi naște din păcat,
Primind o altă lege;
Cu vecinicia sunt legat,
Ci voi să mă dezlege."

"Oh, beautiful you are... In dream
Such demons often appear,
But to this path that's so extreme
I will never get so near.

The strings of my chest are in pain:
Your cruel love absorbs me,
My eyes affliction only gain,
Your sight surrounds and burns me."

"But how thou want me to descend?
The truth is plenty, see me:
I am immortal. Apprehend
That thee are mortal, carefree."

"I'm looking not for mighty words,
I don't know what they might do;
Although your sounds I do record,
I cannot comprehend you.

But if you want indeed that I
With you in love I may be,
Descend to earth, from heaven fly,
And as a mortal take me."

"My immortality thou ask
So that a kiss thou give me,
But so thou know, I take the task
To show how much I love thee.

Oh, yes, in sin I will be born
I will receive a new rite,
With everlasting life I'm sworn,
I'll part from it now in flight."

Şi se tot duce… S-a tot dus.
De dragu-unei copile,
S-a rupt din locul lui de sus,
Pierind mai multe zile.

*

În vremea asta Cătălin,
Viclean copil de casă,
Ce împle cupele cu vin
Mesenilor la masă,

Un paj ce poartă pas cu pas
A-mpărătesii rochii,
Băiat din flori şi de pripas,
Dar îndrăzneţ cu ochii,

Cu obrăjei ca doi bujori
De rumeni, bată-i vina,
Se furişează pânditor
Privind la Cătălina.

Dar ce frumoasă se făcu
Şi mândră, arz-o focul;
Ei Cătălin, acu-i acu
Ca să-ţi încerci norocul.

Şi-n treacăt o cuprinse lin
Într-un ungher degrabă.
– „Da' ce vrei, mări Cătălin?
Ia du-t' de-ţi vezi de treabă."

– „Ce voi? Aş vrea să nu mai stai
Pe gânduri totdeuna,
Să râzi mai bine şi să-mi dai
O gură, numai una."

And he departs… He goes and goes
For love from a young maiden,
Detaching from above he chose,
For days he was as taken.

*

During this time, young Catalin,
Cunning youth at the palace,
Who serves the people at the scene
And fills with wine their chalice,

A page who follows step by step
The queen and holds her garment,
An orphan boy, left on doorstep,
But daring with eyes ardent,

With two young cheeks, fiery red,
Descends onto arena,
He sneaks around and turns his head:
He watches Catalina.

But what a beauty she's become,
And proud… she is so gorgeous…
Well, Catalin, the time has come
For you to check your fortune.

And as in passing, gently, soft,
He corners the young maiden.
"What do you want, boy, are you lost?
Just leave! You are mistaken."

"What do I want?… want you to stop
To always be so thoughtful.
You should be laughing… and then drop
A kiss on my mouth… lawful."

– „Dar nici nu ştiu măcar ce-mi ceri,
Dă-mi pace, fugi departe -
O, de luceafărul din cer
M-a prins un dor de moarte."

– „Dacă nu ştii, ţi-aş arăta
Din bob în bob amorul,
Ci numai nu te mânia,
Ci stai cu binişorul.

Cum vânătoru-ntinde-n crâng
La păsărele laţul,
Când ţi-oi întinde braţul stâng
Să mă cuprinzi cu braţul;

Şi ochii tăi nemişcători
Sub ochii mei rămâie...
De te înalţ de subţiori
Te-nalţă din călcâie;

Când faţa mea se pleacă-n jos,
În sus rămâi cu faţa,
Să ne privim nesăţios
Şi dulce toată viaţa;

Şi ca să-ţi fie pe deplin
Iubirea cunoscută,
Când sărutându-te mă-nclin,
Tu iarăşi mă sărută."

Ea-l asculta pe copilaş
Uimită şi distrasă,
Şi ruşinos şi drăgălaş,
Mai nu vrea, mai se lasă.

"I don't know what you ask of me,
Just go away, run further—
Oh, for the evening star, you see,
My heart is filled with fervor."

"If you don't know, I'll show you clear,
Each step of our love-making,
Just be at ease and do not fear,
It will be quite breathtaking.

Just as the hunter in the grove
For birds prepares his lasso,
When my hand comes to you, my dove,
Your arm comes also narrow.

Your eyes unmoving must remain
Under my eyes, my dear...
And when I lift you up again
Respond to me with cheer.

And if my face to you bends down,
Respond to me with your face,
I will behold you all year-round,
Throughout my life, in all space.

And so you know completely how
To love without a fear,
When kissing you, to you I bow,
You kiss me back, my dear."

She listened closely to the lad
Surprised and quite distracted,
She was attracted, but 'twas bad,
She gave in, she retracted.

Și-i zise-ncet: - „Încă de mic
Te cunoșteam pe tine,
Și guraliv și de nimic,
Te-ai potrivi cu mine...

Dar un luceafăr, răsărit
Din liniștea uitării,
Dă orizont nemărginit
Singurătății mării;

Și tainic genele le plec,
Căci mi le împle plânsul
Când ale apei valuri trec
Călătorind spre dânsul;

Lucește c-un amor nespus
Durerea să-mi alunge,
Dar se înalță tot mai sus,
Ca să nu-l pot ajunge.

Pătrunde trist cu raze reci
Din lumea ce-l desparte...
În veci îl voi iubi și-n veci
Va rămânea departe...

De-aceea zilele îmi sunt
Pustii ca niște stepe,
Dar nopțile-s de-un farmec sfânt
Ce nu-l mai pot pricepe."

– „Tu ești copilă, asta e...
Hai ș-om fugi în lume,
Doar ni s-or pierde urmele
Și nu ne-or ști de nume,

She whispered to him, "I've known you
Quite well, since you a cub were,
Both talkative and untrue:
The two of us may concur…

The evening star emerging, though,
From his full serenity,
Gives a horizon where there's no
More limit to the large sea.

And secretly my lashes bend
For they are filled with tears
When the sea waters to him send
Waves after waves, his peers;

He shines with love that can't be told,
My pain is cured by his beam,
But he goes up, leaving my world,
And I can never reach him.

He penetrates with his cold rays
From a world that I now flee…
Forever I will sing his praise
Forever far will he be…

And thus my days are dry to me,
So dry as in a desert,
But all the nights are holy, see,
A charm I cannot discern."

"You're just a girl… that's all there is…
Let's run the world together.
They'll lose our tracks… Come with me, please,
Our names get lost in aether.

Căci amândoi vom fi cuminți,
Vom fi voioși și teferi,
Vei pierde dorul de părinți
Și visul de luceferi."

*

Porni luceafărul. Creșteau
În cer a lui aripe,
Și căi de mii de ani treceau
În tot atâtea clipe.

Un cer de stele dedesubt,
Deasupra-i cer de stele -
Părea un fulger nentrerupt
Rătăcitor prin ele.

Și din a chaosului văi,
Jur împrejur de sine,
Vedea, ca-n ziua cea de-ntâi,
Cum izvorau lumine;

Cum izvorând îl înconjor
Ca niște mări, de-a-notul...
El zboară, gând purtat de dor,
Pân' piere totul, totul;

Căci unde-ajunge nu-i hotar,
Nici ochi spre a cunoaște,
Și vremea-ncearcă în zadar
Din goluri a se naște.

Nu e nimic și totuși e
O sete care-l soarbe,
E un adânc asemene
Uitării celei oarbe.

For both of us quiet will be,
But also safe and happy,
Your parents you'll forget with me,
And dreams of stars… so sappy."

*

He went. The evening star began
To fly. His wings were growing,
And paths of one thousand years span
Were just some moments flowing.

A sky with spheres was below,
Above, a sky with spheres—
He seemed like bolts that ever-flow,
He wandered through his peers.

And from the valleys of chaos,
And all around his being,
He saw lights springing with pathos
As in the world's beginning.

And as they spring, surrounding him,
Like seas that his swim nourish,
He flies, a thought in love, a beam,
Until all die, all perish.

For where he goes, there is no edge,
Nor eyes, nor grip, and nor souls,
And time attempts to no avail
To come to be from black holes.

There is nothing; still, there is
A thirst that now absorbs him,
A depth akin to an abyss;
Oblivion. No more beam.

– „De greul negrei vecinicii,
Părinte, mă dezleagă
Și lăudat pe veci să fii
Pe-a lumii scară-ntreagă;

O, cere-mi, Doamne, orice preț,
Dar dă-mi o altă soarte,
Căci tu izvor ești de vieți
Și dătător de moarte;

Reia-mi al nemuririi nimb
Și focul din privire,
Și pentru toate dă-mi în schimb
O oră de iubire...

Din chaos, Doamne,-am apărut
Și m-aș întoarce-n chaos...
Și din repaos m-am născut.
Mi-e sete de repaos."

– „Hyperion, ce din genuni
Răsai c-o-ntreagă lume,
Nu cere semne și minuni
Care n-au chip și nume;

Tu vrei un om să te socoți,
Cu ei să te asameni?
Dar piară oamenii cu toți,
S-ar naște iarăși oameni.

Ei numai doar durează-n vânt
Deșerte idealuri -
Când valuri află un mormânt,
Răsar în urmă valuri;

"From my eternity's hard chore,
My father, you release me,
And glorified forever more
In all the world you will be.

Demand from me, Lord, any price,
For a new life from ashes,
For rightly are you spring of lives
But also spring of passes;

Retract from me immortal disk
And fire from my eyeballs,
For just a moment's love I risk
My endless life in your halls.

From chaos, Lord, I have sprung out,
And I'd return to chaos,
And from the rest I'm born, no doubt,
I'm thirsty of some hiatus."

"Hyperion, who from abyss
Arise, the world is in flame,
Don't ask for signs, moments of bliss,
That have no face and no name;

You want as human to comply,
To be like them, in time worn?
But even if all people die,
Again, more people are born.

They last a breath until their doom,
Ideals are to them dear,
When waves in life find their tomb
More waves again do appear.

Ei doar au stele cu noroc
Și prigoniri de soarte,
Noi nu avem nici timp, nici loc,
Și nu cunoaștem moarte.

Din sânul vecinicului ieri
Trăiește azi ce moare,
Un soare de s-ar stinge-n cer
S-aprinde iarăși soare;

Părând pe veci a răsări,
Din urmă moartea-l paște,
Căci toți se nasc spre a muri
Și mor spre a se naște.

Iar tu, Hyperion, rămâi
Oriunde ai apune...
Cere-mi cuvântul meu de-ntâi -
Să-ți dau înțelepciune?

Vrei să dau glas acelei guri,
Ca dup-a ei cântare
Să se ia munții cu păduri
Și insulele-n mare?

Vrei poate-n faptă să arăți
Dreptate și tărie?
Ți-aș da pământul în bucăți
Să-l faci împărăție.

Îți dau catarg lângă catarg,
Oștiri spre a străbate
Pământu-n lung și marea-n larg,
Dar moartea nu se poate...

They just have stars that give them luck,
And their fates' persecutions,
We have no time, no place… We're stuck,
Death's not among our options.

And from the heart of yesterday,
What lives today dies 'morrow,
And if a sun loses its ray
And dies, it's back tomorrow.

It seems eternally to rise,
But death him slowly follows.
For if one's born, one also dies,
And then returns from hollows.

And you, Hyperion, remain,
Regardless of your sunset…
Just ask my first word. Here, it's plain:
Wisdom you want? No regret?

You want me voice to give this mouth
The gift of song, to entice
All mountains, forests, north and south,
So they would follow your price?

You want, perhaps, action to show,
Much strength and also justice?
I'd give you all the earth as though
You are its king, Augustus.

I'll give you fleet, mast next to mast,
All armies if you want, son,
To cross the sea, the earth, so vast,
But death, it cannot be done…

Și pentru cine vrei să mori?
Întoarce-te, te-ndreaptă
Spre-acel pământ rătăcitor
Și vezi ce te așteaptă."

*

În locul lui menit din cer
Hyperion se-ntoarse
Și, ca și-n ziua cea de ieri,
Lumina și-o revarsă.

Căci este sara-n asfințit
Și noaptea o să-nceapă;
Răsare luna liniștit
Și tremurând din apă.

Și împle cu-ale ei scântei
Cărările din crânguri.
Sub șirul lung de mândri tei
Ședeau doi tineri singuri:

– „O, lasă-mi capul meu pe sân,
Iubito, să se culce
Sub raza ochiului senin
Și negrăit de dulce;

Cu farmecul luminii reci
Gândirile străbate-mi,
Revarsă liniște de veci
Pe noaptea mea de patimi.

Și de asupra mea rămâi
Durerea mea de-o curmă,
Căci ești iubirea mea de-ntâi
Și visul meu din urmă."

And if you want to die… for whom?
Just go back, see what is there,
On that earth wandering to doom,
Go and see the whole affair."

*

To his spot given, far away,
Hyperion returned then,
And, just like in the prior day,
His light poured over a ben.

For it is evening, sunset is,
And night is to begin wide;
The moon arises in much peace,
And trembling on the seaside.

And with her sparks it fills the space
In all the small groves' alleys.
Under the crowns of lindens' lace
A lass, her lad were lonely:

"Oh, darling, let my face on yours
Kind bosom find some repose,
Under the eyes' ray that now stores
An untold sweetness of rose.

The sweet delight of your cold light
My thoughts gently refashions,
Eternal silence you do write
On my night filled by passions.

And from above me you remain
And so my pain you cure,
For as my first love you will reign,
My last dream you endure."

Hyperion vedea de sus
Uimirea-n a lor față;
Abia un braț pe gât i-a pus
Și ea l-a prins în brațe…

Miroase florile-argintii
Și cad, o dulce ploaie,
Pe creștetele-a doi copii
Cu plete lungi, bălaie.

Ea, îmbătată de amor,
Ridică ochii. Vede
Luceafărul. Și-ncetișor
Dorințele-i încrede

– „Cobori în jos, luceafăr blând,
Alunecând pe-o rază,
Pătrunde-n codru și în gând,
Norocu-mi luminează!"

El tremură ca alte dăți
În codri și pe dealuri,
Călăuzind singurătăți
De mișcătoare valuri;

Dar nu mai cade ca-n trecut
În mări din tot înaltul
– „Ce-ți pasă ție, chip de lut,
Dac-oi fi eu sau altul?

Trăind în cercul vostru strâmt
Norocul vă petrece,
Ci eu în lumea mea mă simt
Nemuritor și rece."

Hyperion above beheld
The wonder on their faces:
Around her neck an arm he held,
She'mbraced him with her graces…

The silver blooms give their scent
And fall—sweet rain in air—
On these two children. They consent;
Such long and flaxen hair.

And overtaken by her love,
Her eyes she raises. Up there,
The evening star remains above.
Her thoughts depart to his care:

"Descend, oh, gentle evening star,
Upon a beam glide here,
Forest and thought all yours they are,
Transform my luck in cheer!"

He trembles like he did before
On hills and over forest,
Guiding the sea toward its shore,
And waves; alone and modest;

No longer, though, he falls away
In seas as if a lover:
"What do thou care, oh, face of clay,
If it's me or some other…

In narrow circle you relive,
Your luck is daily master,
But I, in my world, always live
Immortal and cold aster."

APPENDIX II

Ageless Youth and Deathless Life

Petre Ispirescu
trans. *Elena Gabor*

Once upon a time, when poplars made pears, when bears had tails, when wolves hugged lambs like brothers, when you could put ninety-nine horseshoes on a flea's legs and it could still jump all the way to the sky to bring us stories, when flies used to write on walls… only liars won't believe the story I'm about to tell you.

Once upon a time, there were an emperor and an empress, both young and handsome. They wanted to have children and tried really hard. The empress visited healers and philosophers, to search into the stars and to divine whether they will have children. Finally, the emperor heard about a wise old man in a nearby village and sent for him. But the wise old man refused to visit the emperor and told the emperor to come to his village instead. And so he did. The emperor, his wife, a few soldiers and servants visited the wise old man. The sage saw them coming and went out to welcome them.

"Why are you here, emperor? What are you looking for? Your wish will bring you sadness."

"I came to ask if you have some medicine to help us have children," said the emperor.

"I do," said the old man. "You will only have one child. He will be Făt-Frumos and loving, but you will not enjoy him."

The empress took the medicine, they returned to the palace, and, in a few days, she was pregnant. Everybody rejoiced at the news. Before being born however, the child started crying incessantly, and no wise man could make him stop. Seeing this, the emperor promised him all the goods in the world, but nothing could make him stop crying.

"Be quiet, my son, and I'll give you this and that land. Be quiet, my dear, and I'll give you a beautiful princess to marry."

Finally, seeing that he wouldn't stop crying, the emperor said, "Quiet, my son, and I'll give you Ageless Youth and Deathless Life."

Then the baby turned silent and was born. All servants and the palace celebrated for a week.

As the baby grew, he became smarter and braver every day. They sent him to schools, and he learned in a month what other children learned in a year. The emperor died and resurrected out of joy. Everyone in the kingdom was proud because they would have a wise and skillful king like King Solomon. Recently, however, the prince was pale and sad, deep in his thoughts. On his fifteenth birthday, the child went to his father who was celebrating with his nobles and servants and said, "Father, the time has come to give me what you promised me at birth." The emperor turned gloomy and told him, "But how can I give you such a thing unheard of? I made you that promise just to get some peace."

"If you cannot give it to me, I am compelled to roam the entire world until I find the promise under which I was born."

All nobles and servants kneeled and begged him to stay. They told him, "Your father is old by now, and we will place you on the throne, and we will bring you the most beautiful queen under the sun as wife."

But nothing could stop him. He remained true to his word, inflexible like a stone. When his father saw his stubbornness, he allowed him to leave and gave orders to prepare him for travel with everything he needed.

Făt-Frumos went to the royal stables that housed the best horses in the kingdom to choose a horse. But, as he pulled their tales, all horses fell down. When he was about to leave, he noticed a thin, sick, old horse in a corner. When he pulled his tail, the horse turned, dug his heels in the ground, and said, "What are your orders, master? Thank God I get to see a brave young man's hand touching me once again."

Făt-Frumos told the horse his plan and the horse said, "To get your wish fulfilled, you need to ask your father for his sword, spear, bow and arrows, and the clothes he wore when he was your age. And you must care for me with your own hands for six weeks, and you must give me barley after you boil it in milk."

Făt-Frumos asked his father for all the things the horse mentioned. Then he called the emperor's butler and asked him to open all the closets so he could choose his clothes. After searching for three days and nights, at the bottom of an old trunk, Făt-Frumos found the rusty weapons and clothes of his father's youth. He started cleaning them and after six weeks they were as shiny as new. He also cared for the horse, as instructed. He worked really hard but succeeded in everything.

When the horse heard that the clothes and weapons were ready, he shook really hard, and all the pustules and wrinkled skin fell off. What was left was a strong handsome stallion, with four wings. When he saw the horse, Făt-Frumos announced, "We leave in three days."

"Yes, master! I'm ready today if you so please," said the horse.

On the third day, the whole palace was deploring his departure. Făt-Frumos, dressed in his father's old clothes, with his father's old sword, on his chosen horse, said goodbye to his father and mother, the nobles, the servants, the soldiers, who, with tears in their eyes, begged him to give up this journey so that he wouldn't end up going toward the ruin of his life. He rode out of the gates like the wind. Following him were two hundred soldiers and a car full of food arranged by his father. Once he was outside the kingdom's borders and reached the wilderness, Făt-Frumos sent the soldiers back, kept only as much food as he could carry and divided the rest among the soldiers.

He faced east and rode for three days until he arrived at a large flat field where he saw many human bones. He stopped to rest, and the horse said: "You know, master, here we are on the land of Gheonoaia, who is so evil, that anyone who sets foot on her land gets killed. She used to be woman like all others, but she was cursed by her own parents because she disobeyed them, and they turned her into Gheonoaia. Right now, she is with her children, but tomorrow she will come to kill you in this forest. She is huge, but don't get scared. Just ready your bow and arrows, as well as your sword and spear if you need them."

They made camp and took turns as lookouts.

Early next day, they were getting ready to cross the forest. He fastened the saddle a little tighter than usual. Then he heard a terrible noise. The horse said, "Hold steady, master. It's her, Gheonoaia."

The trees were falling in her path, she came so fast. The horse flew above her and Făt-Frumos pierced her leg with an arrow. Right when he was aiming the second arrow, she said, "Wait, Făt-Frumos, I won't hurt you. I promise with my blood." She paused. "You got a great horse there, Făt-Frumos. If it weren't for him, I'd have eaten you roasted. But you won. To this day, no mortal dared to cross my land. The few crazy ones who dared to come left their bones on the field you just saw."

They went to her house where she cooked for him and treated him kindly. When Gheonoaia cried in pain from her injured leg, Făt-Frumos put it back together, and it healed right away. Happy, Gheonoaia celebrated for three days and invited Făt-Frumos to choose one of her daughters as his wife. They were all beautiful like fairies. He declined and told her straight what his goal was. She told him, "With this horse and your bravery, I think you'll succeed."

After three days, they started on the road again. They rode for a long, long distance, beyond Gheonoaia's land. They arrived at a beautiful field with green grass on one side and burned grass on the other side.

He asked the horse, "Why is the grass burned?"

"Well, we are on the land of Scorpia, Gheonoaia's sister. They can't live together because of their bad tempers. They were both cursed by their parents, that's why they became animals, like you saw them. They want each other's land and fight over it all the time. When Scorpia is upset, she throws fire and tar. She probably just had a fight with her sister and burned the grass under her. She's meaner than her sister and has three heads. Let's rest a bit, master, and be ready tomorrow morning."

Next day, as they were getting ready, they heard a terrible rattling sound.

"Stay alert, master, Scorpia is coming."

Scorpia rushed towards them swallowing dirt and throwing flames through her huge mouth. The horse flew high above her at an angle, so Făt-Frumos pierced her with an arrow and took one of her heads. Just before cutting another head, Scorpia begged him to spare her and promised peace with her own blood. She welcomed Făt-Frumos into her home and treated him kindly, even better than Gheonoaia. He glued her head back together and healed her. Three days later the prince and his horse were on the road again.

After crossing Scorpia's lands, they traveled for a long, long distance. They arrived at a field full of flowers, where spring ran eternal. Every flower was more beautiful than the next, carrying suave perfumes. The wind was blowing gently. Here they stopped to rest, and the horse said, "We managed to get here, master, but we have one more challenge, a big danger. If we can conquer this too, we'll be ok. A little ahead of us is the palace where Ageless Youth and Deathless Life resides. That palace is surrounded by a thick and tall forest, housing the wildest beasts in the world. Day and night, they're on guard. There is no way to fight them. We can't go through the forest, so we'll try to fly above it. They rested for two days and then got ready. Holding his breath, the horse said, "Tighten the saddle as much as you can, hold on to me tight and don't touch my wings." He flew up and close to the forest. "Master, now is the feeding time for the wild beasts in the forest. Let's go!"

They flew up high and saw the palace shining in the sun. They passed the forest, came down to land on the steps of the palace, and Făt-Frumos barely touched the branch of a tree. Suddenly, the whole forest shook, and the animals started hollering in a most frightening way. Luckily the lady of the palace was outside feeding her "babies" as she called them, and all was alright. She gladly saved them because she had not seen human soul there. She tamed the beasts and sent them away. The Mistress was tall fairy, thin, delightful, and most beautiful!

Făt-Frumos was stunned. The lady of the palace looked at him with pity and said, "Welcome, Făt-Frumos! What are you doing here?"

"We are searching for Ageless Youth and Deathless Life."

"If you're searching for what you said, it is here!"[1]

He entered the palace and found two more women, each as young as the other, the older sisters. He thanked the fairy for saving him, and they cooked for him in golden dishes. They let the horse roam and eat grass wherever he liked and introduced them to the beasts so they could walk in the forest in peace. The women asked Făt-Frumos to live with them because they got tired of being all alone. He didn't need to be asked twice and he received gratefully, since this is what he wanted anyway.

Slowly, they learned each other's ways, and he told them his story and what happened to him until he arrived there, and not long after, he married the youngest sister. When they got married, the other sisters showed him the other parts of the land and told him he can walk anywhere but to avoid one place, the Valley of Tears.

Făt-Frumos spent immemorable time there. He stayed as young as he was when he arrived. He walked through the forest without a care. He enjoyed the comfort of the palace, the love of his wife and his sisters-in-law, and the beauty of the flowers and the sweet, clean air. He was happy. He hunted often. One day, as he was chasing a rabbit, he threw an arrow, then two, but

1 See Noica's discussion in chapter 4 about this. The first "you" is plural, while the second is singular.

missed. Frustrated, he chased it further and finally hit it with his third arrow. Without noticing, he had passed into the Valley of Tears. With the rabbit on his shoulder, he returned home, when he was hit suddenly by a terrible longing for his father and mother. He didn't dare tell the fair women, but they could tell he was sad and restless.

"Unfortunate one, you passed through the Valley of Tears!" they told him utterly scared

"I did, my dears, unintentionally. I am melting because of the longing for my parents, but I cannot bring myself to leave you either. I've spent several days with you here, and I've been very happy. I will go visit my parents one last time, and then I'll return never to leave again."

"Do not leave us, our dear one. Your parents have not been alive for hundreds of years, and, if you go, we are afraid that you will not return. Stay here with us. We have a feeling that you're going to perish if you leave."

Despite the women and the horse pleading with him not to leave, his longing for his parents was inconsolable, and this was withering him completely. Finally, the horse told him, "If you won't listen, master, know that whatever happens it's your fault. I'll tell you something and if you accept my covenant, I'll take you back."

"I accept gratefully. Tell me."

"When we get to your father's palace, I'll drop you off and I'll go back, if you decide to stay even for an hour."

"Alright. So be it," said Făt-Frumos.

They made their preparations, hugged the women, and said their goodbyes, and left them behind sighing and with tears in their eyes. They arrived at the land of Scorpia, where they found cities instead. The forests had changed into plains. He asked around about Scorpia and her house, but they told him that their grandparents heard such stories from their ancestors.

"How is this possible? Only just a short time ago I passed through here." He told people everything he knew and did, but the locals laughed at him and thought he was crazy. Upset, he traveled further, and without his noticing, his beard and hair turned white. He arrived at the land of Gheonoaia, where he asked the same questions that he asked in the land of Scorpia, and he received similar answers. He was baffled. How could things have changed so much in just a few days? Disturbed, he kept on riding. His white beard was now all the way to his waist, and his legs became weak and trembled. He arrived at his father's kingdom where he found different people and new cities and the old ones were so changed that he could no longer recognize them. Finally, he arrived at the palace of his birth. He got off the horse, and the horse kissed his hand and said, "Be well, master, I'll now return to where we came from. If you want to come, get back in the saddle and let's go."

"Go in peace, I also hope to return soon."

The horse darted out of there as fast as an arrow.

When Făt-Frumos saw the abandoned castle with wild plants and weeds all over it, he sighed and, with tears in his eyes, tried to remember the glory days of his childhood, the rooms and halls filled with light. He toured the palace two or three times, looking in every room and corner that reminded him of the past and the stable where he had found the horse. He went down to the cellar, which had its entrance occluded by the rubble.

Looking around, with his white beard all the way to his knees, he had to lift his eyelids with his fingers, and he could barely walk. He found an old trunk. He opened it and saw nothing. Lifting the lid, he heard a weak voice saying, "Finally, you're here. Welcome! If you had been late just a tad longer, I would have died myself."

It was his own Death, who had shriveled so much that she was bent like a hook in the small chest, who slapped him hard. He fell down and turned into ashes on the spot.

Now I'm getting on my saddle, 'cause I'm done telling this fable.

Made in the USA
Coppell, TX
16 March 2024

30172541R10134